EDITOR: LEE JOHNSON

OSPREY MILITARY | **ELITE SERIES** | 56

SCOTTISH UNITS IN THE WORLD WARS

Text by
MIKE CHAPPELL
Colour plates by
MIKE CHAPPELL

D1103603

First published in Great Britain in 1994 by
Osprey, an imprint of Reed Consumer Books Ltd.
Michelin House, 81 Fulham Road,
London SW3 6RB
and Auckland, Melbourne, Singapore and
Toronto

© Copyright 1994 Reed International Books Ltd.

All rights reserved. Apart from any fair dealing for
the purpose of private study, research, criticism or
review, as permitted under the Copyright, Designs
and Patents Act, 1988, no part of this publication
may be reproduced, stored in a retrieval system, or
transmitted in any form or by any means,
electronic, electrical, chemical, mechanical,
optical, photocopying, recording or otherwise,
without the prior permission of the copyright
owner. Enquiries should be addressed to the
Publishers.

ISBN 1 85532 469 5

Filmset in Great Britain by Keyspools Ltd
Printed through Bookbuilders Ltd, Hong Kong

Author's dedication
To the memory of my uncle, 'Robbie' Robertson,
Colour Sergeant in the Gordon Highlanders, and
commissioned into the Hampshire Regiment to fight
alongside the 15th (Scottish) Division in the battle for
the 'Scottish Corridor', Normandy, June/July 1944.

Publisher's note
Readers may wish to study this title in conjunction
with the following Osprey publications:
  MAA 81 *The British Army 1914–18*
  MAA 182 *British Battle Insignia 1914–18*
  MAA 187 *British Battle Insignia 1939–45*
  MAA 112 *British Battledress 1937–61*
  MAA 245 *British Territorial Units 1914–18*
  MAA 120 *Allied Commanders of WW2*

Artist's note
Readers may care to note that the original paintings
from which the colour plates in this book were prepared are available for private sale. All reproduction
copyright whatsoever is retained by the publisher. All
enquiries should be addressed to:
  Mike Chappell
  14 Downlands
  Walmer
  Kent CT14 7XA
The publishers regret that they can enter into no
correspondence upon this matter.

For a catalogue of all books published by Osprey Military
please write to:

**The Marketing Manager,
Consumer Catalogue Department,
Osprey Publishing Ltd,
Michelin House, 81 Fulham Road,
London SW3 6RB**

THE SCOTTISH DIVISIONS IN THE WORLD WARS

THE DIVISIONS

The history of the British Army is rich with the stories of battles fought by small bodies of men in the wars of the past three centuries. Legendary examples are legion: the 'Diehards' fighting to the end at Albuhera; the 28th Foot standing back-to-back to repel the French at Alexandria; the Gordons and the Gurkhas scaling the heights of Dargai, and so on, and so on. Readers of regimental histories might, at times, assume that this or that unit played the major, even the only role in a particular battle, so subjectively are some written.

These sometimes distorted perspectives reflect the pride the British have in their regiments and, perhaps, the insularity which stems from this unique ésprit de corps. Most Britons would argue that this is no bad thing. Pride in regiment has kept generations of British soldiers going

The ruins of Beaumont Hamel after its capture in November 1916. (IWM)

on the battlefields of the world for hundreds of years, helping them to endure the rigours of battle and motivating numerous acts of bravery and self-sacrifice.

The World Wars of 1914–18 and 1939–45 were conflicts on a scale more massive than any the British Army had faced before. During their course, vast operations such as the Somme offensive or the Normandy landings tended to overshadow the contributions of individuals and their units; and in time it became the formation that provided the focus for much of the pride formerly vested in regiments. Both World Wars demanded the nation's resources to the full; this included the conscription of men into the armed forces, and – for the infantry in particular – the consequent dilution and eventual breakdown of the pre-war 'regimental' system, which had guaranteed that a recruit from a particular region could join his county regiment and serve with his fellows. This breakdown made, at times, a charade of the titles worn by individuals. Yorkshiremen who had enlisted into the Green Howards found themselves in battle as Glosters. Ulster riflemen

were sent forward as replacements for the casualties of the Hampshires. Surplus butchers of the Army Service Corps were drafted to the 60th Rifles, and redundant anti-aircraft gunners became infantry at the stroke of a pen.

All, it seems, adapted remarkably well to these transformations, developing a fierce pride in the battalions with which they saw action. But the character of an infantry unit of both World Wars was constantly subject to change as the toll of casualties brought an influx of reinforcements. The heavier the casualties the more the change; and in this atmosphere it became the division that seemed to most to be the constant, their rock of Gibraltar – a self-supporting formation with a commander that every man knew, whose badge was worn by all, and whose exploits and victories were reported in the press for the benefit of the folks at home. For those serving with a very good division there would be the added kudos of the respect and admiration of the rest of the army. Pride in unit, regiment, might remain, but for most it became less important than pride in their division.

The number of divisions raised by Great Britain in the World Wars was enormous by comparison with her modest pre-war regular army: no less than 76 in the Great War, and 61 in the Second World War. Not all of these were to see active service, and those that did experienced a variety of fates. The horrendous casualties suffered by the infantry of the Great War led to certain divisions being 'reduced to cadre'; whilst some divisions in the Middle East were 'Indianised' – having British battalions replaced by Indian – in order to provide reinforcements for the Western Front. The nature of the fighting in the Second World War led to some divisions being disbanded as a result of casualties and losses of equipment, others being broken up to provide reinforcements, and yet others going into captivity as a result of capitulations. There were frequent changes of role as infantry formations were converted to armour of one sort or another, or were trained for some other special type of warfare.

Whatever their circumstances, most British divisions of the World Wars gave good account of themselves; and some so distinguished themselves in battle that they were regarded by their peers as élite formations. Among these were the 18th (Eastern) Division of the Great War, described as 'perhaps the best of all the thirty Kitchener's Army divisions' by Lt.Col. H. Green in his book *Famous Engagements II*. Colonel Green also praises highly the 55th (West Lancashire) Division, a Territorial formation; both divisions gained a reputation for dependability in the attack or the defence. In the Second World War few formations could match the achievements of the 7th Armoured Division, the original 'Desert Rats', from the early battles in North Africa to the crossing of the Rhine. With the 7th for most of their journey was the famed 50th 'Tyne, Tees and Humber' Infantry Division; while two infantry divisions which saw much hard fighting in North Africa and Italy were the 46th (North Midland and West Riding) and the 78th 'Battleaxe' Divisions.

Also regarded highly were those divisions composed of Scottish troops – four during the Great War and three in the Second World War. It is their story that is set out in the following pages.

The battle of the Ancre. German prisoners being counted into the 51st (Highland) Division's cage. (IWM)

THE SCOTTISH SOLDIER

Rifle grenade firing at a skill-at-arms contest. 1/7th Black Watch, 51st (Highland) Division, May 1917. (IWM)

Over the centuries of their existence the Scottish regiments of the British Army have gained a reputation in war that is the envy of all and which can be matched, or surpassed, by very few. Indeed, the very description 'Scottish soldier' conjures up images ranging from the 'thin red streak tipped with a line of steel' of the 93rd Highlanders at Balaclava, and the charge of the Scots Greys at Waterloo, to the more recent deeds of Scottish regiments in the Falkland Islands and the Persian Gulf. The reputation of the martial Scots has been built on a solid foundation of achievement.

Reforms in the late 19th century left the British Army with ten Scottish regiments, and these came to be regarded as five of 'Highlanders' – recruited, broadly speaking, from the northern or highland regions of Scotland and retaining the traditional highland dress – and five of 'Lowlanders'. This organisation remained in being throughout both World Wars.

Not all the men who serve in Scottish regiments are Scotsmen, neither in peace nor war. English lads have enlisted in peacetime as a matter of choice, and have been made welcome, in highland and lowland regiments. In the two World Wars the disparity in population between England and Scotland, and the lottery of infantry reinforcement sent many more Englishmen to Scottish battalions. Once absorbed into the family of a British Army battalion a newcomer rapidly absorbs its atmosphere and the pride that comes from belonging. This is especially so of Scottish battalions, which have always absorbed 'sassenachs' with a minimum of fuss, making them more Scottish than the Scots in no time at all. A story from one of the divisional histories recalls one Lancashire soldier telling another, 'Ah've been a Jock longer than thee!' (Yet another states that by the end of the Second World War Scotsmen were in a minority in units of the division.) The honorary, or 'hostilities only' Scottish soldiers should not be forgotten.

Despite their élite status, battalions of Scottish regiments were rarely grouped together to make up larger formations for war before 1914–18. There had been highland brigades formed at the time of the Crimean War and the Boer War; and brigading had taken place during the Napoleonic Wars which served to group two or more Scottish battalions together. (At Waterloo, for example, Sir Denis Pack's 9th Brigade comprised the 3/1st Foot, Royal Scots; the 1/42nd Foot, Royal Highland Regiment; the 2/44th (East Essex) Regiment of Foot; and the 1/92nd (Highland) Regiment of Foot.) But given the British

Lieutenant-Colonel H. Sutherland DSO, commanding 1/7th Black Watch, May 1917. The Colonel is talking to a Lieutenant of the 1/5th Seaforth Highlanders.

Note the two blue bars of the 1/7th Black Watch and the badge of the 1/5th Seaforth. Both units were with the 51st (Highland) Division. (IWM)

system of raising and employing infantry in battalion 'penny packets' such groupings were random and rare.

It was left to the Territorial Force and the 'Kitchener's' or New Army of the Great War to raise the first divisions composed entirely of Scottish infantry. Two Territorial and two New Army divisions were put into the field for the duration of the war. Following the Armistice of 1918 the Territorial Divisions remained in being to serve throughout the Second World War, alongside one further Scottish division raised for the hostilities.

British infantry organisation, 1908–1914

The British have always disliked the idea of maintaining a large standing army and the compulsory military service that goes with it. In the past money might have been lavished on a navy that made Britain the greatest maritime power in the world, but that spent on the army was

grudgingly given. One of the results was a system of supplementing the infantry of the small standing army by raising extra battalions of volunteers in time of war and cutting them back in time of peace. (It might be argued that the system prevails today. The author's regiment – in the end reduced to a single battalion of perhaps 600 men – after three centuries of overcoming every enemy sent against it in battle, has succumbed at last to the accountant and his balance sheet ... An inglorious end for the 'Glorious Glosters'.)

The system ideally suited the maintenance of a gendarmerie for the British Empire, but was less than perfect when it came to producing an army to fight a major continental war. By the late 19th century the great powers (France, Germany, Russia and Austria) were conscripting the young and able-bodied for military service with the colours, from which they passed to the reserve to be retained until middle age. Conscription created armies that dwarfed that of Britain whilst backing them with a reserve of trained men that ran into millions. By the turn of the century, with the possibility of war with Germany looming, the British government set out to put the nation's army in shape to fight a European war.

Conscription was considered, but rejected as politically unpopular, in favour of a compromise based on the British tradition of voluntary service. The defence of the British Isles was considered best guaranteed by the creation of a Territorial Force founded on the old Volunteer movement, and in 1908 the Territorial and Reserve Forces Act passed into law. Thus the War Office began to create a citizen's reserve army that included 14 divisions and a number of cavalry brigades. Among the former were the Highland Territorial Division and the Lowland Territorial Division, formations that each included 12 battalions of infantry as well as field artillery, engineers, medical services and a divisional train, all recruited from the given divisional area: the highlands of Scotland for the Highland Division, and that part of Scotland south of the line from the Firth of Forth to Loch Lomond for the Lowland Division. Thus came into being the first two Scottish formations, divisions comprised exclusively of Scottish units recruited in Scotland.

The regular battalions of the Scottish regiments were, at this time, disposed at home and abroad and were to enter the war in 1914 in formations that might be described as 'mixed'. That they fought as gallantly as their Territorial and New Army counterparts goes without saying. At least one unit, the 2nd Royal Scots Fusiliers, found itself subsequently posted to a Scottish Division; and three regular battalions found themselves brigaded with a New Army battalion in Macedonia to form a 'Scottish Brigade' (the 1st Royal Scots, the 2nd Camerons, the 1st Argylls, and the 13th Black Watch of the 81st Infantry Brigade). But the story of the regular Scottish infantry is not that of the Scottish divisions in the Great War.

On the outbreak of war in August 1914 Lord Kitchener was appointed Secretary of State for War. An autocratic figure, considered throughout the Empire to be Britain's most able military man, Kitchener declared that the war would last for three years and that Britain required 70 divisions to fight it. His view contradicted the popular assumption that the war would be a brief affair, but such was his stature that the call went out on 7 August for the first volunteers to fill the divisions of 'Kitchener's Army'. By the middle of September 1914 half a million men had enlisted.

Kitchener decided that his New Army had to be organised as a separate entity from the Regular and Territorial Armies, and organised his New Army divisions into groups of six – 9th to 14th, 15th to 20th, and so on. There was, apparently, some indecision as to what units were to be called; one faction favoured simply numbering the battalions. Kitchener declared himself to be uninterested, 'as long as we get the men'. In the end it was decided to raise units as additional battalions of the regiments of the infantry of the line. The early New Army battalions for the Scottish regiments were formed together in what became the 9th (Scottish) Division of the First New Army. Later battalions were formed into the 15th (Scottish) Division of the Second New Army. By the time subsequent New Army formations came to be formed the allocation of units to Scottish, Irish, Northern, Eastern, Western and Light divisions had been dropped, and grouping reverted to the regular army practice of selecting whoever was available.

SCOTTISH DIVISIONS IN THE GREAT WAR

The 51st (Highland) Division, 1914–18

(The division, a 'first-line' formation of the Territorial Force, was entitled the 1st Highland Territorial Division until 12 May 1915, when it was numbered as the 51st. A 2nd Highland Territorial Division began forming from 31 August 1914; termed 'reserve' or second line, it was eventually numbered as the 64th (2nd/Highland) Division. It remained in defence of the United Kingdom throughout the war, finding reinforcements for the first line.)

Units of the division had just completed their annual camps when the order was issued on 4 August 1914 to mobilise for war, following which the 1st Highland Territorial Division concentrated in the Bedford area. The troops of the division are recorded as having been 'among the earliest to volunteer for active service abroad'; and it is interesting to note that between mobilisation and May 1915, when the 1st Highland Territorial Division crossed to France, no fewer than six battalions of infantry, the Highland Mountain Artillery Brigade, a Field Company and a Field Ambulance had left the division to reinforce formations abroad. (With them went two battalions, the 4th and 5th, from the Black Watch Brigade. Four Territorial battalions of this regiment had been allocated as Army Troops.) Their replacements altered the character of the infantry brigades in particular. These had been the Argyll

Bombers' of the 1/5th Seaforths march past at a parade of the 51st (Highland) Division, August 1917. Note the wearing of shorts, the single red bar on the sleeves, and the 'bombers' grenade badges. (IWM)

51st (Highland) Division

(As at November 1916)
G.O.C.
MAJOR-GENERAL G.M. HARPER

152nd Infantry Brigade	153rd Infantry Brigade	154th Infantry Brigade	Pioneers
1/5th (Sutherland & Caithness) Bn. Seaforth Highlanders	1/6th (Perthshire) Bn. Black Watch	1/9th (Highlanders) Bn. Royal Scots	1/8th Bn. Royal Scots
1/6th (Morayshire) Bn. Seaforth Highlanders	1/7th (Fife) Bn. Black Watch	1/4th (Ross Highland) Bn. Seaforth Highlanders	
1/6th (Banff & Donside) Bn. Gordon Highlanders	1/5th (Buch & Formatin) Bn. Gordon Highlanders	1/4th Bn. Argyll & Sutherland - Highlanders	
1/8th (Argyllshire) Bn. Argyll & Sutherland Highlanders	1/7th (Deeside Highland) Bn. Gordon Highlanders	1/7th Bn. Royal Scots	

The 'HD' Highland Division – sign was sometimes depicted as above, and sometimes in full block letters. It rapidly became one of the best-known divisional signs in the BEF.

and Sutherland Infantry Brigade – 6th, 7th, 8th and 9th Battalions; the Gordons Infantry Brigade – 4th, 5th, 6th and 7th Battalions; and the Seaforth and Cameron Brigade – 4th, 5th and 6th Seaforths and 4th Camerons. They went to France with the 6th and 7th Black Watch and four battalions of English infantry. In time the English were replaced as original battalions found their way back to the divisional fold, or other Highland Territorial units were posted in.

In reserve at 'Second Ypres', the 51st (Highland) Division participated in its first battles at Festubert in May 1915 and Givenchy in June 1915, after which it moved south to the Somme sector to take over parts of the line from French troops and the Indian Cavalry Division. It was here in September that the command of the division was assumed by Maj.Gen. G. M. Harper, the General Officer Commanding who was to lead the division until March 1918.

In March 1916 the 51st (Highland) Division was again on the move, this time north to the Labyrinth, a

General Maxse, the Corps Commander, presents medals to men of the 51st (Highland) Division, August 1917. The Lance Corporal signaller is from the 1/5th Seaforths and the Company Sergeant Major and Sergeant from the 1/6th Seaforth. Note the three different bonnet badges, the red bars on the sleeves and the gas helmet haversacks worn as sporrans. (IWM)

sector of the line extending from Neuville St. Vaast to Roclincourt where it again when into the line to relieve French troops. Here the 51st were subject to increasing enemy harassment which included persistent mining – the digging of tunnels beneath a position, packing them with explosive and then detonating the 'mines' to devastate the trenches above them. The firing of these devices was followed by an immediate assault. The 1/6th Argylls suffered particularly in these operations, becoming so depleted in numbers that they were withdrawn from the division.

On 12 July 1916 the division moved south to the Somme once more, where the great offensive launched on 1 July was raging with bitter intensity. At this time, for all its losses, the 51st (Highland) Division was 'still largely composed of pre-war, non-conscript, old Scottish territorials', and is recorded as being 'at the very top of its form'. (It should be noted that conscription had by now been introduced in Great Britain, and from its introduction the old, volunteer character of the British Army began to be diluted.) Such was the composition and morale of the troops of the division as they entered the series of battles that lasted from July to November 1916, and which have come to be known as the 'Battle of the Somme'.

On the night of 22/23 July, 154th Infantry Brigade of the 51st (Highland) Division went into action as part of a concerted attack by troops of three divisions on High Wood. In the van were two battalions of the Brigade, the 1/4th Gordons and the 1/9th Royal Scots – the 'Dandy Ninth', a Territorial highland battalion of the Royal Scots. Despite fierce hand-to-hand fighting both battalions were repulsed, losing 450 men in the process. It was a bitter introduction to the Somme battles; but it was to be the

The massed pipes and drums of the 152nd Infantry Brigade, 51st (Highland) Division, August 1917. On parade are the 1/5th and 1/6th Seaforths, the 1/6th Gordons and the 1/8th Argylls. (IWM)

closing battle of this grim campaign that was to establish the 51st (Highland) Division as an élite formation, and caused one commentator to record that by 1917 the 51st was 'perhaps the best not only amongst the Territorial divisions in France, but in the whole Army'.

The so-called Battle of the Ancre and the capture of Beaumont Hamel took place between 13 and 19 November 1916. The aim of the operation was to reduce the head of the German salient south of Serre and astride the Ancre stream, a series of strongpoints that had resisted all attempts at their capture since 1 July. North of the Ancre the assault was to be delivered by the 63rd (Royal Naval), 51st (Highland) and 2nd and 3rd (Regular) Divisions. Facing the 51st were strong defences including the 'Y' Ravine salient, beyond which was the fortified village of Beaumont Hamel. The assaulting formations were the 153rd Infantry Brigade on the right (1/7th Gordons and 1/6th Black Watch assault battalions, 1/5th Gordons support and 1/7th Black Watch finding carrying parties) and the 152nd Infantry Brigade on the left (1/5th Seaforth and 1/8th Argylls assault battalions, 1/6th Seaforths support and 1/6th Gordons in reserve). The 154th Infantry Brigade was in divisional reserve.

Zero hour was an hour and a half before sunrise, 5.45a.m., and was signalled by the blowing of a mine of 30,000lbs. of high explosive on the front of the 152nd Brigade and the opening of the supporting artillery barrage. The assault started well. On the right the 1/7th

Gordons followed the barrage, capturing the German front trenches, and reached the first objective by 6.45a.m. With the enemy retiring before them the assaulting companies pressed forward before consolidating their position. On their left the 1/6th Black Watch were held up by the 'Y' Ravine salient. (The ravine, thirty feet deep, with sides that were almost perpendicular and with tunnels connecting with the neighbouring trenches, was a formidable obstacle.) Up from support came the 1/5th Gordons, and the position was by-passed by groups of the 1/6th Black Watch who pushed on.

As dawn broke a heavy fog shrouded the battlefield making observation from the rear and from the air impossible; but reports of the situation were reaching divisional headquarters, enabling the GOC to send forward reinforcements, including the 1/4th Gordons, when and where required. Under pressure from the grenades and bayonets of the highlanders surrounding them, the Germans in the 'Y' Ravine position surrendered and the assault pressed on. Early in the afternoon a mixed group of the 1/4th and 1/5th Gordons and the 1/6th Black Watch entered the southern end of Beaumont Hamel, to find troops from the four battalions of the 152nd Infantry Brigade were also there.

The 1/5th Seaforth and 1/8th Argylls had had a hard fight for the German front trenches. The support line was not so difficult, but deep mud and the loss of the barrage meant that reinforcements from the 1/6th Seaforth and 1/6th Gordons were needed before the German reserve line could be carried and the advance pressed on to Beaumont Hamel. Here it took most of the afternoon fighting through the ruins to clear the Germans from their positions in dug-outs and cellars. This done, the first objective

had been reached and consolidation was carried out. Two tanks had been sent forward to assist in the assault, but both became 'ditched'.

The following day, the 14th, saw units of the 51st (Highland) Division patrolling forward, with little progress being made as confusion over orders and shelling from British batteries created chaos. On 15 November the dispersing mists made observation possible, and the 1/7th Argylls were ordered to attack a position called Frankfort Trench in concert with units of the 2nd Division. Despite being shelled before they started and then running into their own barrage, parties of the Argylls broke into their objective, only to be forced to withdraw to their jump-off point. On the 16th there was little activity, and on the 17th began the relief of the 51st (Highland) Division.

The fight through 'Y' Ravine and on to the capture of Beaumont Hamel over ground 'horrible with the dead, and the litter of the struggle in the previous July', was conducted with a highland élan described as 'irresistible'. In the words of their Corps commander, it was 'one of the greatest feats of the war', and to those who know the ground and its defences it must ever be a marvellously fine performance'. Between 6,000 and 7,000 prisoners were taken by the 51st (Highland) Division. It is altogether fitting that a statue of a highland soldier stands today in the Beaumont Hamel Memorial Park as a tribute to the division's achievements there.

After a further period in trenches the highlanders left the valley of the Somme, having sustained 8,000 casualties in the battles of 1916. They were next in the line at Arras where, after a period of intensive training, they took part in the series of battles fought from 9 April to 16 May 1917 that go under the collective name of the Battle of Arras.

The battle of Cambrai. Men of the 51st (Highland) Division with German prisoners, 20 November 1917. (IWM)

The 51st (Highland) Division fought at the first and second battles of the Scarpe and the capture and defence of Roeux.

On the morning of 9 April the division, in concert with the 9th and 15th (Scottish) Divisions, attacked on the right of the Canadian Corps assault on Vimy Ridge, and in the teeth of a German barrage, to seize the enemy positions with the aid of tanks. The first day of the Arras battle delivered a devastating blow to the Germans, whose losses included 13,000 prisoners and a large quantity of guns and equipment. The gains, measured in miles in some places, were greater than anything so far achieved. There followed a series of stubbornly-fought actions with the enemy counter-attacking after every gain by the British, and culminating on 15 and 16 May with the defence of Roeux by the 51st despite being nearly encircled. Congratulations for this feat were sent by Gen. Allenby, the Army commander, and by the Corps commander.

At the end of May the division moved north towards yet another offensive, 'Third Ypres', the campaign more commonly known by the name of the village reached as the offensive spent itself – Passchendaele. On the morning of 31 July 1917 the 51st (Highland) Division advanced to seize their objective – the line of the Steenbeck – overcoming the opposition of pill-boxes and beating off the inevitable counter-attacks in the battle of Pilkem Ridge. (It was in this attack that Sgt. Alexander Edwards of the 1/6th Seaforths won his Victoria Cross when a German machine-gun pinned down his company. Edwards attacked the machine-gun post, killed the gunners and captured the gun. Later, though wounded, he stalked and killed a sniper, rescued a wounded officer and led his men on to

their objective. A second Victoria Cross was won this day by Pte. George McIntosh of the 1/6th Gordons.)

On 20 September the division again went forward in the battle for the Menin Road Ridge, with the same degree of success. The Corps commander expressed his appreciation for 'the thoroughness of organisation within the Division, and the fact that all usual war problems have been thought out beforehand, discussed in detail, and are embodied in simple doctrines well known to all ranks. The result is the Division always fights with gallantry, and can be depended on to carry out any reasonable task which may be allotted to it in any battle. For this reason I venture to place it among the three best fighting divisions I have met in France during the past three years'.

By mid-November the 51st were in the Cambrai sector, and about to become involved in the Battle of Cambrai. This opened on 20 November 1917 when seven British divisions supported by 324 tanks achieved a major break in the German lines with the first massed tank attack ever launched. The 51st (Highland) Division had as its objective the fortified village of Flesquières. Despite the availability of tank support the commander and staff of the 51st considered the ground 'rendered the co-operation of the tanks unsatisfactory', and the division went unsupported by them. (It was on the opening day of the battle that L/Cpl. Robert MacBeath of the 1/5th Seaforth, a Lewis gunner, was detailed to 'reconnoitre', and went forward to put five enemy machine-guns out of action and to capture 33 of the enemy. He was awarded the Victoria Cross.) Despite severe casualties the infantry had, by nightfall, worked their way around Flesquières, which fell to them next day; they then pressed on three miles to seize

Walking wounded of the 51st (Highland) Division awaiting evacuation, April 1918. (IWM)

Cantaing, and 500 prisoners, finally capturing Fontaine-Notre-Dame with the aid of tanks and cavalry. The next day a German counter-attack regained Fontaine, and heavy casualties were sustained by the division in trying to retake it on 23 November. On 30 November the Germans, heavily reinforced, launched a series of counter-attacks which cancelled out the British gains and ended the series of battles in stalemate. But the courage and dash shown by the 51st (Highland) Division in the first days of the battle once again earned the admiration of all and the plaudits of the Corps commander.

In March 1918 the GOC, Maj.Gen. Harper, was promoted to a Corps and command of the division was assumed by Maj.Gen. G.T.C. Carter-Campbell. General Harper had led the division through a momentous period and was affectionately known as 'Uncle' Harper by all. (The HD monogram of the divisional sign was irreverently said to stand for 'Harper's Duds' at one time. At the time of his leaving few would quarrel that the division was Harper's, but it would have been an ill-informed person who referred to his command as duds.)

The 51st (Highland) Division were in the line in the Bapaume area when the bombardment that was to precede the German attacks of 21 March 1918 began. This was to be the final enemy attempt to win the war, and they hurled the divisions released by the collapse of the Russians against the thinly-stretched British Army on the Somme. The part of the line held by the 51st was 5,400 yards wide and 4,000 yards deep. The divisional infantry battalions had recently been cut from 12 to nine, and were deployed with none in reserve. Facing the 51st were elements of eight German divisions.

The barrage, when it broke, lasted for five hours before the infantry attack was launched. For three days the troops of the 51st (Highland) Division fought stubbornly to cling to their positions, and then fought a series of rearguard actions as they withdrew, suffering nearly 5,000 casualties as they did so. (It was during this desperate fighting that Lt. J.C. Buchan of the 1/7th Argylls won a Victoria Cross.) At the end of March, as the division left to join the First Army, their former Army commander recorded their 'splendid conduct – they have broken up overwhelming attacks and prevented the enemy gaining his objective – namely, a decisive victory'.

Sent to Flanders to refit and receive reinforcements, the division was again called for to stem the German attack from Aubers Ridge, an intervention that cost the 51st over 3,000 casualties. Sent to the Champagne region in July to operate alongside the French, troops of the division once again found themselves in the path of a German offensive. This time they were able to join in the counter-attack on the common enemy, but the three weeks' fighting cost nearly 3,500 men. Among them was Sgt. John Meikle of the 1st/4th Seaforth who, on 20 July, advanced alone armed with only a revolver and a stick, to knock out two enemy machine-guns. He was killed attacking a third gun and was awarded a posthumous Victoria Cross.

Sent north once again, the 51st fought a series of battles as they advanced against an enemy who had shot his bolt but was determined to fight to the end. In August the division captured Greenland Hill, and in October pushed the enemy back ten miles with a series of attacks. These final battles of the 51st (Highland) Division's war cost nearly 3,000 casualties, and saw another officer, Lt. William Bissett of the 1/6th Argylls, win the Victoria Cross.

On 29 October 1918 the division – less artillery – was withdrawn into Army Reserve, and on 11 November the Armistice was signed. The 51st (Highland) Division had fought its last battle in the Great War. The total cost in casualties had been over 27,000 men.

In February 1919 three battalions of the Division were detached for duties with the Army of the Rhine and a different Highland Division, one formed only for occupation duties. Demobilisation proceeded, and by mid-March

THE WESTERN FRONT

1919 the division had been 'reduced to cadre'. In 1920 the 51st (Highland) Division was re-formed in Scotland, where it continued in the peacetime role of a Territorial Army formation until the start of the Second World War.

The 52nd (Lowland) Division, 1914–18

The 1908 Haldane reform of the Volunteers and Yeomanry into the Territorial Force brought into being what became known as the 2nd Lowland Territorial Division. The order for general mobilisation issued on 4 August 1914 reached the headquarters of the Lowland Division at 5.25p.m., and began the train of events that was to take the division to the battlefields of the Dardanelles, Palestine and the Western Front. Before that journey began, however, the division deployed to defend its home area in accordance with its war role. Armed with obsolete weapons and equipped with commandeered transport, units of the Lowland Division dug trenches, set up barbed wire, and stood guard against a possible invasion.

Under the existing law this was all the Territorial Force could be called upon to do; but on 10 August 1914 Lord Kitchener, the Secretary of State for War, called for complete units of Territorials to volunteer for service overseas. Within days the majority of men of the division had volunteered, and a 'second line' was set up for each unit into which the non-volunteer element was transferred. (This had the effect of creating a 2/2nd Lowland Territorial Division, causing the original division to become the 1/2nd.) Whilst this reorganisation was taking place men continued to enlist into the Territorial Force; thus the ranks of both the 'first-line' and the 'second-line' were filled.

In November 1914 units of the division began to be sent to France to reinforce the hard-pressed British Expeditionary Force. (First to go was the 1/9th HLI, the Glasgow Highlanders, followed by the 1/5th and 1/6th Scottish Rifles. Their places were taken by the 1/5th Argylls, 1/4th Royal Scots and 1/7th Royal Scots.) In April 1915 the 1/2nd Lowland Division was warned for overseas, and on 7 May its destination was revealed – the Dardanelles. There an expeditionary force had landed at Gallipoli intent on knocking Turkey out of the war, but were now in difficulties and in need of support. The Lowland Division was to be part of that reinforcement, and embarkation for the Dardanelles began on 18 May.

It was at this time that two events occurred that are forever associated with the division. The first was a change to the title it would make famous in two World Wars. From 11 May 1915 the division became the 52nd (Lowland) Division, its infantry brigades becoming the 155th, 156th and 157th instead of South Scottish, Scottish Rifles and Highland Light Infantry.

Troops of a battalion of the KOSB in trenches on the Helles front, 1915. The scene is typical of the conditions endured by units of the 52nd (Lowland) Division at Gallipoli. (IWM)

The second event was the involvement of a unit of the division in one of the most terrible railway disasters of all time. On 22 May 1915 500 officers and men of the 1/7th Royal Scots, travelling south for embarkation, were involved in a multiple train collision near Gretna which resulted in an uncontrollable fire. Only seven officers and 57 men survived uninjured. The remaining two companies of the 1/7th, travelling in a separate train, formed the basis for the reconstituted battalion, which was brought up to strength with volunteers from the 8th HLI.

On 29 May 1915 the first units of the 52nd (Lowland) Division began to land at Cape Helles, Gallipoli, and by 3 July the three infantry brigades, two field ambulances and two howitzer batteries were ashore. The situation they found was one of stalemate. The first British landings in April had as their aim the seizure of the ground commanding the passage of warships to the Sea of Marmara and Constantinople. Far from achieving this, the British were contained in two beachheads by the Turks and were having to pay dearly for every inch of ground. Suffering from shortages of water and artillery ammunition, the British were outnumbered by the enemy, dependent on naval gunfire for support, and increasingly weakened by sickness. (The supply of water, ammunition and rations was difficult in the extreme. These had to be brought to the beaches in small craft and then manhandled forward under Turkish observation and fire.)

The first troops of the 52nd (Lowland) Division went into the line on 9 June 1915. (The 5th Royal Scots Fusiliers, 850 strong, found themselves relieving a unit reduced by casualties and sickness to 250 men.) Each brigade, as it came ashore, went forward to relieve units in the line to receive 'instruction' in the type of trench warfare being waged in the Gallipoli peninsula.

52nd (Lowland Division)

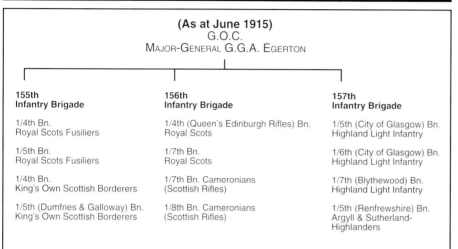

(As at June 1915)
G.O.C.
MAJOR-GENERAL G.G.A. EGERTON

155th Infantry Brigade	156th Infantry Brigade	157th Infantry Brigade
1/4th Bn. Royal Scots Fusiliers	1/4th (Queen's Edinburgh Rifles) Bn. Royal Scots	1/5th (City of Glasgow) Bn. Highland Light Infantry
1/5th Bn. Royal Scots Fusiliers	1/7th Bn. Royal Scots	1/6th (City of Glasgow) Bn. Highland Light Infantry
1/4th Bn. King's Own Scottish Borderers	1/7th Bn. Cameronians (Scottish Rifles)	1/7th (Blythewood) Bn. Highland Light Infantry
1/5th (Dumfries & Galloway) Bn. King's Own Scottish Borderers	1/8th Bn. Cameronians (Scottish Rifles)	1/5th (Renfrewshire) Bn. Argyll & Sutherland-Highlanders

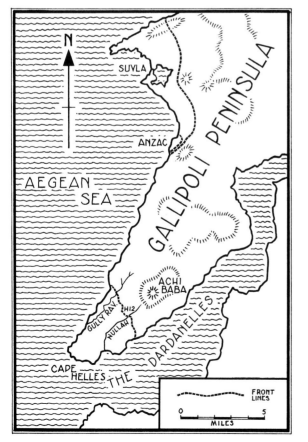

The divisional sign of the 52nd (Lowland) Division was not devised until the last year of the Great War.

Its 'L' stood for Lowland and it featured the shield of St Andrew upon which was a thistle.

On 28 June the British launched an attack against the Turkish right. Elements of two divisions and an independent brigade took part in the battle of Gully Ravine, including the 156th Infantry Brigade from the 52nd (Lowland) Division (the 1/7th and 1/8th Scottish Rifles and 1/4th and 1/7th Royal Scots, the latter still seriously under strength). The 155th Infantry Brigade was in reserve.

When the British barrage commenced at 9a.m. Turkish artillery and machine-guns opened fire on the trenches sheltering the assault troops, causing severe casualties before the attack began. The British artillery fire on the front of the 156th Brigade was so ineffective as to cause the Turks little concern; when the assault was ordered at 11.02a.m. the units of the brigade sprang into the open without 'the slightest hesitation on the part of any battalion', and into a storm of Turkish rifle and machine-gun fire, with the shrapnel 'coming down like hail'.

On the left, men of the 1/4th Royal Scots began to fall as soon as they left the shelter of their trenches; but the others pressed on, obeying the order not to shoot but to use the bayonet, and stormed the Turkish front trench. Reduced even further in numbers, they advanced on the second Turkish trench line; backed by a third wave, the assault waves took the second line and advanced on yet another line of Turkish trenches. By now nearly every officer had been killed or wounded, but men such as CSM Lowe of the 1/4th Royal Scots led their companies on to seize and hold objectives (CSM Lowe was awarded the Distinguished Conduct Medal).

On the right, however, disaster befell the 1/8th Scottish Rifles, who attempted to attack a Turkish strongpoint of six to eight machine-guns which had been untouched by the British bombardment. They were 'slaughtered by platoons'. An attempt by the 1/7th Scottish Rifles to take this position met with the same fate. (This position, 'H12', was to remain in the hands of the Turks until the end of the campaign despite many further attempts to take it.) The losses were appalling. Before the battle the strength of the headquarters and battalions of the 156th Infantry Brigade had been 2,941 all ranks; the casualties sustained amounted to 1,563 killed, wounded or missing – a 53% loss – which included the brigade commander, Brig.Gen. W. Scott-Moncrieff among the dead.

Despite the heroic failure to take the 'H12' feature the battle resulted in one of the greatest victories ever won on Gallipoli. Gains were more than expected, especially on the British left by the 29th Division and the Gurkhas. The lack of howitzers and sufficient ammunition prevented the British from capitalising on the gains of 28 June, but there was no doubting that Turkish morale had been severely shaken. Despite this they counter-attacked at Helles and at Anzac (the second lodgement), only to be bloodily repulsed. Their losses for the period 28 June–5 July were estimated at 5,000 killed and 15,000 wounded.

The survivors of the 156th Infantry Brigade were formed into two composite battalions, one each of Royal Scots and Scottish Rifles. There was much recrimination as to where the blame lay for the failure of the British barrage and the inability of units sent against 'H12' to effect its capture. One thing was never in doubt: the courage of the men of the Royal Scots and Scottish Rifles battalions of the 156th Brigade. In their first battle they had borne the Turkish bombardment until zero hour, and had then gone forward with the bayonet against an enemy fully alerted and waiting for them. All who witnessed their conduct expressed admiration for gallantry on such a scale.

In July the Turks reinforced their army in the Gallipoli peninsula and began a series of attacks against the British positions. Their form was to advance en masse, and an officer of the 7/8th Scottish Rifles noted that 'in shooting them down we got some of our own back'.

By now all the brigades of the 52nd (Lowland) Division were established at Helles and ready to play their part in the next attack on the Turks, which was planned to draw enemy attention away from the impending British landings at Suvla Bay. The troops of the 52nd taking part in the attack were from the 155th and 157th Infantry Brigades, and their orders were to advance and capture three lines of trenches to the centre of the enemy position at Achi Baba Nullah.

At 4.30a.m. on 12 July 1915 fire was opened on the objectives of the 155th Brigade (1/4th Royal Scots Fusiliers and 1/4th and 1/5th KOSB) by field artillery and naval gunfire, and later by small arms fire from the 157th Brigade on the left. At 7.35a.m. the lines of Borderers and Fusiliers climbed out of their trenches and advanced on the Turks with fixed bayonets. Once again they were lashed by enemy fire, but they broke into the Turkish trenches, taking the first and second lines and pushing on

Turkish rifles and ammunition salvaged after the battle of Gully Ravine, 29 June 1915. (IWM)

to what appeared to be the third trench, their given objective. By the time it was realised that no third trench existed it was impossible to issue orders for all to retire, and some groups of the 1/4th KOSB were seen advancing deeper into enemy territory. Those who did turn back came under fire from their own guns as well as those of the enemy; the battalion was all but wiped out, losing 550 of the 700 men who had gone over the parapets that morning.

But the main Turkish position had been taken, and now followed fighting to hold and consolidate what had been gained. Forward came companies of the 1/5th Royal Scots Fusiliers, the remains of the 1/4th, the 1/7th Royal Scots and 1/7th Scottish Rifles. Meanwhile, on the left, the 157th Infantry Brigade waited to play its part.

Artillery had been firing on the objective of the brigade all day, but at 1550 hrs. commenced an intense hour-long bombardment, following which the 157th climbed onto their parapets and, to the skirl of the pipes, went forward. Wave after wave of the brigade's infantry (the 1/6th and 1/7th HLI and the 1/5th Argylls) strode on through Turkish fire to capture the first and second lines of enemy trenches – and to advance on the non-existent third. Again confusion reigned; men were lost when no third line was found, and much bitter fighting ensued to consolidate and hold the positions won. In this the companies of the 1/5th HLI, called forward, performed valuable work.

In terms of the fighting at Gallipoli a victory had been won in the operations of 12–13 July. Once again serious casualties had been inflicted upon the Turks, and their morale was again dashed. But the cost had been great: of a strength of 10,900 men landed the 52nd had suffered 4,800 casualties up to 13 July. The lowlanders had acquitted

Troops of the 52nd (Lowland) Division marching to the beach for a 'bathing parade' at Gallipoli, 1915. (IWM)

themselves nobly in their first battles; but little by little, man by man, the fine volunteer spirit of the division was weakened as the pre-war Territorials became casualties and were replaced by wartime volunteers and, eventually, conscripts.

And so, for the remainder of the year, the men of the 52nd endured the thirst and the flies, the squalor and discomfort of life on the Helles front, as well as the mayhem visited on them by the Turks. In July the 4th (Glasgow) Howitzer Battery was sent to Anzac to join the division's 5th Battery and to support the lodgements there and at Sulva. On 13 August Pte. D. Ross Lauder of the 1/4th Royal Scots Fusiliers won the first Victoria Cross awarded to a man of the 52nd (Lowland) Division when he smothered a grenade in a trench. The onset of winter in November only served to exchange the miseries previously suffered for those of rain, cold and frost, and did not affect the intensity of the fighting, with the British mounting a series of attacks in which units of the 52nd (Lowland) Division played their part.

By now it was obvious to all that the Dardanelles expedition could not succeed in its aim. A visit from Lord Kitchener resulted in the decision to evacuate; the positions at Sulva and Anzac were given up on 20 December 1915, and the Helles front was evacuated on 9 January 1916. If the British conduct of the campaign at Gallipoli gave cause for criticism, the manner of their leaving did not. Regarded today as a classic of deception, the evacuations were carried out without alerting the Turks and without the loss of a single man.

The total losses in battle for the British (including Imperial and Colonial) Army at Gallipoli have been reckoned at 117,549. The 52nd (Lowland) Division had lost 70% of its officers and 50% of its men killed, wounded or missing. (These figures do not include hospital admission for sickness.) It has been said that the Dardanelles under-

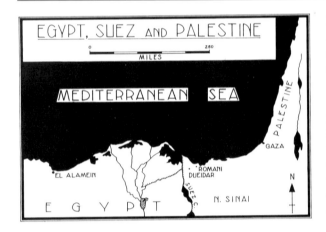

EGYPT, SUEZ AND PALESTINE

MEDITERRANEAN SEA

taking was brilliant in concept, and might have brought about an earlier Allied victory had more men, more guns and more ammunition been committed from the start. What was never lacking was fortitude and courage.

After the evacuation the units of the 52nd (Lowland) Division were shipped to Egypt where, after the division's assembly, they were reinforced, re-equipped, and sent once more to face 'Johnny Turk' across the wastes of Sinai in defence of the Suez Canal. The first clash with the enemy was at Dueidar in April when the 1/4th and 1/5th Royal Scots Fusiliers beat off a determined attack. In August the 52nd, together with the ANZAC Mounted Division, were again in action at the Battle of Romani, where a Turkish force was defeated and put to flight with losses of 5,000 killed and wounded and 3,930 taken prisoner. (Of 49 officers captured 25 were Germans or Austrians, and an entire German machine-gun company was taken.) By early 1917 an advance across the northern Sinai had the British poised for the invasion of Palestine, which began with the First Battle of Gaza in March. At this the 52nd (Lowland) Division was in reserve. The Second

Battle of Gaza began on 17 April with an assault on the Muntar fortress, and was marked for the division by the desperate assault on Outpost Hill on the 19th. British casualties for the battle are given as 7,000, of which 2,000 were lost by the 52nd.

The British repulse at Second Gaza was followed by a period of trench warfare before the town during which 2nd Lt. J.M. Craig, 1/5th KOSB, won the Victoria Cross for rescuing wounded under fire. By October 1917, with Gen. Allenby now in command of the 'Egyptian Expeditionary Force', preparations were made for the capture of Gaza and the series of battles that were to lead to the defeat of the Turks. Gaza was taken at the third attempt by 7 November, and the 52nd went on to fight at Wadi el Hesi, Burqa, El Maghar, the capture of Junction Station, the Battle of Nebi Samweil, the Battle of Jaffa and the Passage of the Nahr el Auja. (On 1 December 2nd Lt. J. Boughey, 1/5th Royal Scots Fusiliers, won a posthumous Victoria Cross in a furious grenade fight at El Burj.) In March 1918 the division was ordered to the Western Front, and left the Middle East.

By 23 April 1918 the 52nd (Lowland) Division had concentrated in France. In early May it took over part of the line near Vimy, and in July it was withdrawn into GHQ Reserve prior to what has been termed 'The Advance to Victory'. In August the division participated in the battle that led to the breaking of the Hindenburg (Siegfried) Line about Hénin Hill (in which battle Lt. D.L. MacIntyre, Adjutant of the 1/6th HLI, won the Victoria Cross); and between 31 August and 3 September broke through the Drocourt-Quéant line. Throughout September, October and right up to the ceasefire of 11 November the 52nd (Lowland) Division played a major role in the

Infantry of the 52nd (Lowland) Division going forward, September 1918. (IWM)

Left: This private of the KOSB shows the typical uniform worn during the Great War by 'Lowland' infantry. Only the 'Tam-o' -Shanter' bonnet and insignia distinguished them as Scots.

Above: A young soldier of the 6th Highland Light Infantry in the Mackenzie kilt worn by this battalion. (P. Hannon)

British advance, crossing the Canal du Nord and ending the war near Mons. (In these final weeks of fighting another Victoria Cross was won when Cpl. D.F. Hunter of the 1/5th HLI, with six of his men, held out in a forward post for 96 hours until relieved.)

So ended the story of the 52nd (Lowland) Division in the Great War. Among its many honours and awards perhaps the greatest accolade was paid by the Germans, who drew up a table of those British divisions their troops were said to hold most in 'dread': on a list headed by the 51st (Highland) Division, the 52nd (Lowland) Division was fourth. Demobilisation reduced units 'to cadre' one by one as the division in France dwindled away. In 1920 it was re-formed again in its home area of Scotland.

The 9th (Scottish) Division, 1914–18

In August 1914 the volunteers who flocked to Scotland's recruiting offices in response to Lord Kitchener's call were enlisted into the New Army for 'three years or the duration of the war'; then packed off to regimental depots to be issued with whatever uniforms, arms and equipment were available, and formed into 'service' battalions of their regiments. Taking the Black Watch (Royal Highlanders) as an example: the 1st and 2nd Battalions were of regulars, the 3rd a reserve for the first two, and the 4th to 7th Battalions of the Territorial Force. The 8th (Service) Battalion, therefore, was the first of the New Army battalions of the regiment. Formed at the Black Watch depot at

The thistle of Scotland, painted in blue, adorned the signboards and vehicles of the 9th (Scottish) Division for over two years before it was worn on uniform, in white metal on a blue disc of cloth.

9th (Scottish) Division

(As at July 1916)
G.O.C.
MAJOR-GENERAL W.T. FURSE

26th (Highland) Infantry Brigade	27th Infantry Brigade	South African Infantry Brigade	Pioneers
8th (Service) Bn. Black Watch	11th (Service) Bn. Royal Scots	1st South African Infantry	9th (Service) Bn. Seaforth-Highlanders
7th (Service) Bn. Seaforth Highlanders	12th (Service) Bn. Royal Scots	2nd South African Infantry	
5th (Service) Bn. Queen's Own-Cameron Highlanders	6th (Service) Bn. King's Own-Scottish Borderers	3rd South African Infantry	
	9th (Service) Bn. Cameronians (Scottish Rifles)	4th South African Infantry (South African Scottish)	

Perth. the battalion was sent to Aldershot on 21 August, a mere ten days after the publication of Kitchener's appeal.

In September 1914 the units that were to form the Scottish Division of 'Kitchener's first hundred thousand', or 'K1', began to assemble in the Bordon area, one of the satellites of the military town and barrack complex of Aldershot, to undergo the training that was to turn them into a fighting formation.

These were not the sort of units, the type of recruits, that the British Army was accustomed to. They have been described as the pick of the nation, the very best of the patriotic youth of the time. The standard of physique was exceptionally high, as were the standards of education and intelligence, and they threw themselves into the routine of training with energy and good humour. But energy was a poor substitute for the shortages that existed in instructors, arms and stores, and these continued to retard progress towards efficiency. Much time was spent at musketry on the numerous rifle ranges of the area, and many trench systems were dug for practice. Route marches, 'manoeuvres' and 'divisional field days' went to make up the training of the division which, by the spring of 1915, was considered ready to go to France. On 8 May 1915 advance parties began to leave for the front. Only eight months had elapsed since the troop trains brought the raw recruits of the division south, and now the 9th (Scottish) Division, the senior 'Kitchener' division, was off to war. (The division had been numbered as the 9th in August 1914 and its infantry brigades as the 26th (Highland), 27th and 28th.)

By 15 May the division had concentrated at St. Omer, from where its units moved to undergo instruction in the realities of warfare at the front, mainly under the wing of

the 6th (Regular) Division. Spells in the line at Armentières were interspersed with instruction in bombing, rifle grenades, mortars, and the many techniques of existing in and fighting from trenches. By 1 July the 9th (Scottish) Division, being considered fit for the role, relieved the 7th (Regular) Division in the line at Festubert, where six weeks of enduring enemy shelling, patrolling and an inspection by Lord Kitchener completed the division's introduction to the Western Front.

On 2 September the 9th took over a section of the front near Vermelles, and were warned to prepare for their part in an attack that was to be mounted later in the month. The Russians were under pressure in the east, and a joint Anglo-French offensive was to be mounted to relieve that pressure. The British were to attack at Loos, and the protection of the northern flank was to be the role of the 9th (Scottish) Division. Still lacking sufficient artillery support for the venture, the British were pinning their hopes on the use of gas.

Four days of artillery bombardment, feint attacks and machine-gun barrages preceded the release of the chlorine gas from 1,200 cylinders on 25 September at 5.50a.m.; and 40 minutes later the assault battalions of the division left their trenches and advanced towards their objectives, four battalions in three lines – the 10th HLI, 6th KOSB, 5th Camerons and 7th Seaforth.

On the left the unbroken enemy wire brought the attack to a standstill, and the intense fire poured upon the attacking battalions and those sent to support them caused such fearful casualties that the 28th Infantry Brigade, the assault formation, lost two-thirds of its strength. On the right the 7th Seaforth broke into the Hohenzollern Redoubt and carried its objective. The 5th Camerons, however, came under such an intense fire that, although they reached their objective, only two officers and 70 men were left of the 820 who had gone over the parapet.

By now the supporting battalions of the 26th (Highland) and the 27th Infantry Brigades were following up, taking severe casualties as they crossed the open ground; but the captured positions were reached, and work went ahead to consolidate the division's gains in the face of enemy shelling and counter-attacks. By the evening of the 25th orders were received that the positions won were to be handed over to troops of the 24th Division, a 'K3' New Army formation which had been in France barely four weeks and was in trenches for the first time. Subsequent German counter-attacks regained most of the ground lost to the 9th (Scottish) Division, despite valiant efforts in support of the 24th Division by units of the 9th. (In this fighting the GOC, Maj.Gen. G.H. Thesiger, was killed, and Cpl. James Pollock of the 5th Camerons won the Victoria Cross for his part in the defence of the Hohenzollern Redoubt.)

Its first battle had cost the 9th (Scottish) Division dear – 190 officers and 5,867 men; but the morale of the division remained unshaken, the survivors feeling that they had met the German and had his measure. The failures at Loos were ascribed to shortages of ammunition and material, the gas, the inefficiency of British bombs and mortars, and the inexperience of the New Army divisions. This last criticism could not be applied to the 9th, whose

gallantry and self-sacrifice were praised officially by the Corps commander, and unofficially by all who witnessed the battle.

The division moved to Ypres and began to repair the damage wrought by Loos. Maj.Gen. W.T. Furse took command of the division, and eight new infantry battalion commanders were posted in to replace those lost. Reinforcements were absorbed, and the 9th settled down to the dangers and discomforts of the Salient, which included a gas attack just before the division left the Ypres front on 20 December 1915.

A period of rest and retraining followed, during which Winston Churchill arrived to take command of the 6th Royal Scots Fusiliers. (As First Lord of the Admiralty Churchill had been the chief architect of the Gallipoli venture. With the failure of his plan, he had resigned his office and sought a command at the front. He went home again in May 1916.) In late January 1916 the division was again in trenches, this time in the 'Plugstreet' Wood area. It was here, in this rather quiet sector of the front, that reorganisation took place when the divisional artillery was restructured, trench mortars were re-deployed, and the infantry of the division underwent drastic upheaval, with the posting out of four of the battalions to the 15th (Scottish) Division, the breaking up of the 28th Infantry Brigade, and the posting in of the South African Brigade. The divisional cavalry were posted away, as were the cyclists. Sundry other goings and comings went to com-

plete a thorough shakedown. In May 1916, the 9th (Scottish) Division received orders to move south to the Somme, where a great Allied offensive was about to be mounted.

On 1 July, along a 25-mile length of the Somme front, 14 British and three French divisions went into the attack, to be repulsed, in the British sector, with the worst casualties ever suffered by a British army. Only in the south, where the British line met the French, were there gains; and it was here on 3 July that the 9th (Scottish) Division was ordered to relieve the 30th Division before Montauban. The first units of the division in action were those of the 27th Infantry Brigade ordered to capture Bernafay Wood. This they did for the loss of only six men, while capturing 17 prisoners, three guns and three machine-guns.

On 14 July the 9th (Scottish) Division went into the attack in what has been termed the Battle of Bazentin Ridge. The divisional objectives were to seize the German positions in Longueval and occupy Delville Wood and Waterlot Farm. At 3.25a.m. the division jumped off with the 26th (Highland) Infantry Brigade on the right (the 8th Black Watch and 10th Argylls) and the 27th Infantry Brigade on the left (the 11th and 9th Royal Scots). Following a creeping barrage the assaulting battalions on the right overcame all opposition; but those on the left were stopped by enemy fire before the second objective had been reached. Strong enemy reaction now halted the advance, and a series of fights developed as units attempted to get forward to their objectives. At 6.15a.m. on 15 July the South African Brigade, preceded by a barrage, advanced into Delville Wood and captured all but the north-west portion. Having taken the position the South Africans and Scots now fought for three days to hold it, and to evict the Germans from their toe-hold; but on 18 July an enemy counter-attack regained parts of Delville Wood and Longueval. (It was on this day that Pte. W. Faulds of the 1st South African Infantry won the Victoria Cross for rescuing an officer under fire.) On 19 July the 9th (Scottish) Division was relieved; since 1 July the division had lost 314 officers and 7,303 men, mostly from its infantry battalions, but it had not fought in vain, retaining nearly all the ground it had won and establishing a reputation as one of the hardest-fighting formations in France. The Army Commander said 'The attack and capture of . . . the village of Longueval on the 14th July was a feat of arms which will rank high among the best military attainments of the British Army, whilst in the capture of Delville Wood, the gallantry, perseverance and determination of the South African Brigade deserves the highest commendation'.

After Longueval the units of the division were rested and re-equipped before absorbing the small drafts of reinforcements available to them. In August the 9th (Scottish) Division were back in the line at Vimy Ridge; but on 25 September they began the move back to the Somme and the battle that was raging there.

Early in October the division was again in action at

Left: The battle of Bazentin Ridge, July 1916. Survivors of the 9th (Scottish) Division returning from the fight for Longueval and Delville Wood. These men are from the battalions of the 26th (Highland) Infantry Brigade. (IWM)

Right: Men of the South African Scottish serving with the 9th (Scottish) Division, in trenches on Frezenberg Ridge, September 1917. (IWM)

the Battle of the Transloy Ridges, when attacks were mounted against the positions around the Butte de Warlencourt, a sinister hill of chalk beside the Bapaume road. The hill and its surroundings had been heavily fortified by the Germans, and the fighting took place in abysmal weather and in a sea of mud which, at times, made movement all but impossible. A few small gains were made for a great deal of sacrifice in what has been described as the most dismal of all the 9th (Scottish) Division's battles. The Butte remained impregnable, resisting all British attempts at its capture.

In November the division left the Somme, and in December went into the line at Arras. It was here, in April 1917, that the 9th were again involved in an offensive. At 5.30a.m. on 9 April the British barrage crashed down upon the German lines, and following it as it advanced by lifts ten British divisions went into the attack on a front of ten miles. It was Easter Sunday – a day of bitter cold and driving sleet. In the centre of the offensive, astride the River Scarpe, three Scottish divisions and one English division with a Scottish infantry brigade attacked in concert: the 51st (Highland) Division, 34th Division (with a brigade of Tyneside Scots), 9th and 15th (Scottish) Divisions. The units of the 9th (Scottish) Division fought their way forward along the north bank of the Scarpe in grand style, to secure all their objectives along with over 2,000 prisoners, 17 pieces of artillery, 24 machine-guns and three trench mortars. The skilled use of artillery, tanks, mortars and machine-guns combined with better training, command and communications came together on 9 April to produce 'a very great triumph for British arms', which included the capture of Vimy Ridge by the Canadian Corps to the north as well as the gains made on the Scarpe. After the triumph of the first day, the 9th fought in a series of battles around Roeux and Greenland Hill that marked the limits of the British advance.

Moved to the Somme once more in June, the division left that area to move to Ypres, where a British offensive had been going on since July. By the time the 9th (Scottish) Division was committed to 'Third Ypres' the battlefield resembled a series of fortified ridges in a vast lagoon of mud; and it was one of these ridges that the division strove to capture on 20 September 1917. In the action near Frezenberg that day two Victoria Crosses were won by men of the 9th – Capt. H. Reynolds of the 12th Royal Scots, and L/Cpl. H. Hewitt of the 2nd South African Infantry – in attacks on the concrete 'pillbox' machine-gun posts that the Germans had made the keystones of their defence works. The units of the 9th (Scottish) Division secured their objectives and were relieved four days later. On 12 October the division was involved in the battle for the approaches to the village that was to give its name to the whole campaign – Passchendaele. Assault battalions floundered forward through the mud at zero hour, into ground that drowned several men who were unfortunate enough to fall into shell-holes, and clogged rifles and machine-guns into uselessness. Most units got no further than 100 yards from their jump-off points; and

The South African Brigade that served with the 9th (Scottish) Division comprised of a 'South African Scottish' battalion and three South African Infantry battalions. Here, the uniforms of both are illustrated by men of the South African Brigade, 1917. (IWM)

here they remained until relieved on 24 October. In early December the 9th (Scottish) Division was rushed to the Cambrai area where a German breakthrough was feared.

March 1918 found the division in the line before Gouzeaucourt east of Bapaume, where the German offensive, launched on the 21st, forced the 9th into a fighting withdrawal in which a large part of the South African Brigade was cut off and wiped out, fighting to the last. By 26 March the fighting strength of the division had been reduced to 1,340 men, and two days later they were withdrawn from the line. The 9th (Scottish) Division had gone down fighting, and had earned the admiration of friend and foe alike. By their dogged resistance the men of the division had bought the time needed to stem the German advance, whilst extracting a heavy toll of the enemy. They had significantly helped to save the British Army from a disaster, earning the praise of Sir Douglas Haig: 'Great gallantry has been shown by the troops engaged in the fighting – the 19th and the 9th Divisions have distinguished themselves by the valour of their defence.'

After absorbing reinforcements the 9th (Scottish) Division went into the line south of Ypres in April, in time to play a part in the halting of the German offensive at

A private of the 6th KOSB, 9th (Scottish) Division.

Men of the 8th Seaforths, 15th (Scottish) Division, carrying forward defence stores, 16 September 1916. Martinpuich had been captured the day before and now work was in hand to consolidate the gains.

23

Casualties of the 9th (Scottish) Division, Meteren, August 1918.

Note the silver thistle divisional signs which were by now being worn. (IWM)

Wytschaete and Kemmel. Once again the division distinguished itself, and once again the Commander in Chief singled it out for praise.

By now the German attempt to win a quick victory was spent, and the Allies gathered their strength for the series of battles known as the Advance to Victory. These lasted from August until 11 November 1918, and the 9th (Scottish) Division was well to the fore in the fighting that forced the Germans back and led them to sue for an armistice. Three more Victoria Crosses were won by men of the 9th during this period: Lt. R.V. Gorle of the 5th Brigade, Royal Field Artillery; Pte. T. Ricketts of the Royal Newfoundland Regiment (then serving with the division's 28th Infantry Brigade); and Cpl. R. Elcock of the 11th Royal Scots.

On 4 December 1918 troops of the division entered Germany as part of the force sent to establish a 'watch on the Rhine'. Here, in 1919, demobilisation began; and on 16 March the 9th (Scottish) Division – after certain movements of units – was renamed the Lowland Division. It had been a long road from Bordon to the Cologne Bridgehead, and along the way the 9th had won a great reputation as a hard-fighting division. It had also lost 52,055 men killed, wounded and missing.

The 15th (Scottish) Division, 1914–18

The 15th was the Scottish division of 'K2', Lord Kitchener's second hundred thousand volunteers, and it was recruited in much the same manner as already described for the 9th (Scottish) Division.

By mid-September 1914 the men who were to form the 15th (Scottish) Division had been sent to Aldershot, and the difficult task of creating the division had begun. What had been available in the way of experienced officers and NCOs, clothing, equipment and arms had been allocated to the units and formations of 'K1', leaving very little for the 15th. Scarcely a unit had more than a commanding officer, an adjutant and a quartermaster. The 7th Royal Scots Fusiliers had only a recently-commissioned quartermaster-sergeant to supervise the turning of 900 men into a fighting unit. There was great discomfort to be endured, through a lack of accommodation and bedding and a low standard of food. An air of muddle prevailed, with leaders being chosen from men with a smarter appearance than their fellows, and 'officers' learning the evening before what they were to teach their men the following day.

On 26 September the 15th paraded for inspection by their King. 'The whole division was in plain clothes. Some wore straw hats, others caps and bowlers. Men clad in well-cut suits stood next to others in workmen's clothes.' But an atmosphere of enthusiasm prevailed throughout

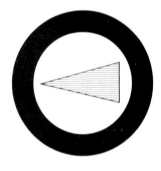

15th (Scottish) Division

(As at September 1915)
G.O.C.
MAJOR-GENERAL F.W.N. McCRACKEN

44th Infantry Brigade	45th Infantry Brigade	46th Infantry Brigade	Pioneers
9th (Service) Bn. Black Watch	13th (Service) Bn. Royal Scots	7th (Service) Bn. King's Own-Scottish Borderers	9th (Service) Bn. Gordon Highlanders
8th (Service) Bn. Seaforth Highlanders	7th (Service) Bn. Royal Scots Fusiliers	8th (Service) Bn. King's Own-Scottish Borderers	
10th (Service) Bn. Gordon Highlanders	6th (Service) Bn. Queen's Own-Cameron Highlanders	10th (Service) Bn. Cameronians (Scottish Rifles)	
7th (Service) Bn. Queen's Own-Cameron Highlanders	11th (Service) Bn. Argyll & Sutherland Highlanders	12th (Service) Bn. Highland Light Infantry	

The divisional sign of the 15th (Scottish) Division was the letter 'O' – the fifteenth of the alphabet – enclosing a wheel 'scotch' in divisional red. Hence – 15th-scotch-division.

the ranks, a keenness quite unlike anything experienced by a British Army before, and this was to carry the division through the trials of the early days. One of these was the first issue of uniform, when items of 'full dress', scarlet tunics and blue trousers, added to the ridiculous appearance of units on parade. In lieu of headdress 'caps, comforter', woollen stocking caps, were issued as the 'crowning absurdity'.

In November units of the division were sent out of Aldershot to satellite camps and billets, and in February 1915 even further afield to the Salisbury Plain area. Chronic shortages were still hampering training, only being resolved in the early summer when items such as Lewis guns, signalling equipment and new personal equipment appeared. But if things were bad for the infantry they were doubly so for the artillery and engineers of the division, who had horses but no harness, and only dummy or obsolete guns to train with. Only by early July, when the 15th was warned for France, were the units of the division fully equipped.

The 8th Black Watch, 15th (Scottish) Division, march back from the capture of Martinpuich, September 1916. (IWM)

By mid-July the 15th (Scottish) Division had crossed to France, moved to the Bethune area, and had begun instruction in trench warfare under the guidance of the 47th (London) Division. By 3 August the 15th had relieved this division in the line. Units of the division were now required to labour mightily in the task of putting their trenches and wire in good order while suffering the harassment of enemy shelling and patrol activity, and the constant round of learning the new skills of trench warfare.

By the end of August the first indications of an impending attack were received. In what would come to be known as the Battle of Loos the 15th (Scottish) Division was given the task of capturing the high ground north of Loisons-sous-Lens. The attack was to be preceded by a four-day artillery bombardment of the German lines and, at zero hour, the discharge of gas. The operation was originally planned for 10 September 1915, but was twice postponed, until 25 September. There was a great deal of preparation to be undertaken, including the digging of over 13,000 yards of communication trenches and the carrying forward of tons of stores and ammunition.

At 6.30a.m. on the 25th the leading companies of the assault battalions climbed the parapets of their trenches and followed the clouds of chlorine gas and smoke towards the German positions. Leaking gas cylinders had un-

Pipe Majors and Drum Majors of the 15th (Scottish) Division, May 1917. The variety of 'tribal' distinctions are evident in this photograph. Tartans, badges and customs of dress.

nerved some of the men in the vicinity of Piper D. Laidlaw of the 7th KOSB; to steady them Laidlaw climbed onto the parapet in spite of enemy fire and marched up and down playing 'Scotland the Brave' on his pipes. His courage and example had an immediate effect, and his company dashed out to the assault. Laidlaw continued playing until wounded; he was awarded the Victoria Cross, and gained fame as 'the piper of Loos'.

The fire that the British faced now intensified, especially the rifle and machine-gun fire, but the conduct of the troops of the 15th (Scottish) Division was such that an observer commented: 'It was magnificent. I could not have imagined, that troops with a bare 12 months training behind them could have accomplished it.' On they marched through a storm of cross-fire, and took possession of the ruins of the German front-line trenches. From here the assaulting columns pressed on to Loos village, where fierce hand-to-hand and house-to-house fighting took place.

By now casualties had thinned the ranks of the assaulting battalions – the 9th Black Watch, 8th Seaforth, 10th Scottish Rifles and 7th KOSB – and supporting battalions had come up to reinforce the attack, including the 10th Gordons and 7th Camerons. By 8a.m. troops of the division had begun to advance up the western and north-western slopes of Hill 70, but had by now outstripped the formations on their right and left and had exposed their flanks, especially on the left. At 8.45a.m. Hill 70 was taken; the remnants of the assault battalions, by now inextricably mixed and with most of their officers casualties, pressed forward ' with the utmost power of the

Officers and men of the 15th (Scottish) Division at a horse show, May 1917.

Note the divisional sign, the 'scotch', painted on the side of the wagon. (IWM)

division' as they had been ordered, and met the full force of the German retaliation as they mounted a counter-attack to regain Hill 70. Driven back, the men of the 15th attempted to hold a line below the western crest of the hill and, despite pressure on both flanks and heavy losses, all seemed well. Here another Victoria Cross was won, by 2nd Lt. F. Johnson, 73rd Field Company, Royal Engineers for rallying the men and leading charges.

At 2p.m. the 21st Division was ordered to reinforce the troops of the 15th now clinging to their gains. The Scots had broken through four lines of German trenches to a depth of over 3,000 yards, and had lost 75 per cent of their fighting strength in doing so. At 9p.m. Maj.Gen. McCracken, GOC of the 15th, received orders to attack Hill 70 on the following morning; and after a night of rain and German counter-attacks the attack went in at 9a.m., only to be halted a few yards out from the British trenches. The CO of the 6th Camerons, Lt.Col. A. Douglas-Hamilton, gathered together the remnants of his battalion to lead them four times against Hill 70 until killed at their head; he was awarded a posthumous Victoria Cross, and Pte. R. Dunsire of the 13th Royal Scots also won the VC at this time.

When the units on the left of the 15th (Scottish) Division fell back a galling fire was opened from that flank. An attack by troops of the 21st Division was broken up by enemy artillery, following which the Germans commenced an advance that forced the survivors of the 15th to aban-

don their positions on the slopes of Hill 70 and to withdraw into Loos By this time some British units were in utter confusion, with leaderless troops returning and dismounted cavalry having to be sent forward to restore the situation. On 27 September the 15th (Scottish) Division was withdrawn from the line.

The series of actions that went to make up the Battle of Loos went on until 4 November. In this fighting two of the 'Kitchener' divisions, the 21st and 24th, were to lose over 8,000 men from an attacking strength of under 10,000 – an appalling figure. Equally appalling were the losses of the 15th (Scottish) Division, mostly sustained on the first day: killed, wounded, missing and gassed, the total came to 6,404, mostly from the infantry. The four assault battalions mentioned earlier lost 679, 700, 625 and 656 respectively.

The battle was hailed as a victory at the time, but it is difficult to justify it as such today. What cannot be denied is the courage, fighting spirit and tenacity demonstrated by the men of the 15th (Scottish) Division in the battle. Few would deny that they were sent into their first (and in most cases, only) battle ill-prepared and poorly supported, but their conduct throughout reflected great credit on them and on the division.

Men of the 8/10th Gordons, 15th (Scottish) Division, using a trench periscope, September 1917. Note the gas alarm klaxon horn on the trench wall. (IWM)

Right: Concert party of the 15th (Scottish) Division, 1917. Note the insignia worn by the sergeant (see colour plate E). (IWM)

After Loos the 15th went into Corps Reserve and began reorganisation, which included absorbing 4,000 reinforcements, after which it went back into the line on 19 October. (It was at this time that Sgt. J. Raynes of the 71st Brigade, Royal Field Artillery won the Victoria Cross for saving life.) The division was to stay in this area, sustaining the usual drain of casualties from trench fighting, until July 1916, when it marched south towards the Somme.

In August 1916 the 15th (Scottish) Division went into trenches near Martinpuich, and on the 12th of the month were ordered into the attack against German positions south of Martinpuich. This took place following a four-day bombardment and was delivered at night, the assault battalions jumping-off at 10.32p.m. – and meeting a German attack in no-man's land. This stopped the 12th HLI, who sustained over 200 casualties, but the Scots Fusiliers and Camerons of the 45th Infantry Brigade were able to capture the German trenches. Over the next few days units of the division pressed on with a series of local attacks that pushed the British front line nearer Martinpuich, which was attacked on 15 September, captured, and consolidated: 'a better conceived and better executed operation it would be difficult to find. Artillery, engineers and infantry worked together in a manner little

short of marvellous – a serious blow had been dealt to the enemy'.

After Martinpuich the 15th (Scottish) Division was withdrawn into Corps Reserve. By this time Scotland's well of manpower was running dry, and the divisional history records that reinforcements included 'men from all parts of England and Scotland'. By early October, with rest and refitting completed, the division moved back into the line as the weather worsened and torrential rain turned the shell-torn battlefields and rear areas into vast bogs. To the hazards and discomforts of manning trenches was now added the misery of cold and mud; and it was under these conditions that men of the 15th existed until February 1917, when they left the Somme area and marched north to Arras.

Mention has already been made of the part played by the Scottish divisions in the Battle of Arras. The 15th (Scottish) Division went into the attack on 9 April on the right of the 9th (Scottish) Division with the River Scarpe as the inter-divisional boundary. The assault brigades were the 44th and the 45th, with four battalions 'up': the 8/10 Gordons, 9th Black Watch, 6/7th Royal Scots Fusiliers and 11th Argylls. Jumping off at 5.30a.m. behind an intensive barrage, the assault battalions fought their way onto their second objectives by noon, allowing the 46th Infantry Brigade to pass through to seize the final objective of the division by 4p.m. At 6.30p.m. the 37th Division passed through the gains of the 15th (Scottish) Division to continue the attack. All this had been achieved by much hard fighting in bitterly cold weather; 500 prisoners had been taken by the division, as well as over 40 guns and numerous machine-guns – 9 April 1917 had been a day of triumph for the 15th (Scottish) Division. But the story of the division at Arras from this point on is the same as for all the British formations involved. German reaction bogged the offensive down in a series of costly battles that gained little compared to the first day. The 15th were sent forward again on 11 April – in a snowstorm – and yet again on 23 April against German positions at Monchy and Guemappe. When relieved on 28 April the division were able to reckon their losses over the 19 days fighting at 6,313 men killed, wounded and missing.

The division was now allowed to 'rest' until the middle of June, when it moved to the Ypres front. There, after periods in the line, the 15th (Scottish) Division was once again involved in an offensive – later to be called 'Third Ypres' or 'Passchendaele' – when it fought in the battles of Pilckem Ridge, Langemarck and Zevencote. In September 1917 the division left Ypres and travelled south to Arras, leaving behind the mud, the good comrades lost and the bitter fighting of the salient. Their former Army Commander sent them off with the following message: 'The Commander of the Fifth Army bids good-bye to the Fifteenth Division with great regret. Its reputation has been earned on many battlefields, and has never stood higher than now. He wishes it all good fortune and many further successes in the future. "Will ye no' come back again?" ' General Gough could have had little appreciation of the effect of his message and the response it would elicit (the most printable being, 'No bloody fear!').

The division remained in the Arras area over the winter of 1917/18, and was in the Monchy area when the German offensive of 21 March 1918 was launched. The enemy gains to the south of the Arras area forced the 15th to withdraw, and a German attack on the positions of the division was beaten back on the 24th. On 28 March another attack turned the right flank of the division and it fell back, fighting, to what was termed the Army Line and the defence of Arras. The German attack had been contained, at a cost to the 15th (Scottish) Division of over 5,000 casualties in eight days fighting.

The division remained near Arras until ordered south to the Marne in July as one of a group of four British divisions which included the 51st (Highland) Division. On 23 July the 15th went into the attack in the first of a series of battles aimed at assisting the French and American

formations in the area. In early August the division moved back to the Arras area where orders were received on the 21st to move to Loos, scene of the division's first battle.

The British positions at Loos had changed since the division's last stay, and were held by means of 'defended localities' – an idea copied from the Germans – reached by tunnels in which had been dug kitchens, hospitals, sleeping accommodation, etc., lit by electricity. The whole system was a complete contrast to the crowded ditches up which men of the 15th (Scottish) Division had struggled under fire to reach the assault trenches in September 1915.

In early October the Germans before the Loos position began to withdraw and a pursuit was mounted in which the units of the 15th played their part, harrying the enemy across the River Scheldt to reach a position south of Ath when the cease-fire was ordered on 11 November 1918.

It was the end for the 15th (Scottish) Division. Demobilisation began in December; the division dwindled as units were reduced to cadres and equipment guards, and on 27 June 1919 the division passed out of existence and into history. It left behind a list of battle honours that began with Loos and ended with the Advance to Victory; and 45,542 men of the division killed, wounded and missing in the acquisition of those honours.

THE SECOND WORLD WAR

British infantry organisation, 1939–1940

Determined not to repeat the administrative blunders of 1914, the British War Office set out plans for mobilisation that, in the event, worked well in the run-up to war in 1939. Following the period of tension created by the Munich crisis of 1938 the Territorial Army was virtually doubled in size as units were 'duplicated' to create extra infantry, armoured and anti-aircraft units. Conscription began before the outbreak of hostilities with the call-up for service of the first 'Militia Men' in 1939.

The Territorial Army of 1938/39 was a different organisation to the Territorial Force of 1914, which volunteers had joined for service within the boundaries of the United Kingdom. At that time only those opting for 'imperial service' could be required to serve overseas, and this led to difficulties in units in which men stuck to their conditions of enlistment and refused to be coerced into volunteering to serve abroad. The problem had been tackled in August 1914 when orders were issued to sepa-

Officers of the 15th (Scottish) Division celebrate Hogmanay, 1917. (IWM)

Men of the 7th Argylls, 51st (Highland) Division, in France June 1940. Note the system of saltires and bars worn on battledress.

rate the home-service men from the imperial service men and to form the former into 'reserve' or second-line units. This measure was to apply to all units in which 60% or more of the strength had volunteered for active service abroad. However, very many units elected for imperial service to a man, and these were soon in action. But the duality of commitment led to bad feeling in the army as a whole, and this was not confined to junior ranks. For refusing to consider the Territorial Force as a structure through which a general mobilisation could be effected, Kitchener has been criticised as failing to make use of an obvious resource. The growing-pains of his New Army were very real, with the volunteers who flocked to his call lacking just about everything required to build an army.

The 'three-army' chaos of 1914 – Regular, New and Territorial – did not prevail in 1939, when every officer and man was deemed to be part of the British Army from the point of mobilisation. This 'embodied' the 51st (Highland) Infantry Division and the 52nd (Lowland) Infantry Division and brought them onto a war footing, as well as the 'duplicates' of these divisions, the 9th (Highland) Infantry Division and the 15th (Scottish) Infantry Division. These were to be the Scottish divisions of the Second World War.

Great War divisions were designated by a number, a subsidiary title and the word 'Division'. Only cavalry or mounted divisions were given a supplementary title. In the Second World War, with the advent of armoured divisions, airborne divisions, mixed divisions, county divisions, etc., the supplementary title 'Infantry Division' was deemed necessary.

The 51st (Highland) Infantry Division, 1939-45

In the aftermath of the Great War Britain cut back her armed forces to the strengths she was accustomed to keeping in peacetime. The huge citizen army was dismantled as men were demobilised and units disbanded, and in this rush to disarm, units of the old Territorial Force were disposed of with the rest.

In 1920 it was decided to raise once more the Territorial Force (renamed the Territorial Army in 1921) to the establishment of 1914, and to recruit for 14 divisions. These were to bear the numbers allocated to them in the Great War; and so it was that the 51st (Highland) Division, Territorial Army, sprang to life as the inheritor of the tradition of its Territorial Force predecessor.

For almost 20 years the men who dedicated their spare time to the 'TA' endured the jibe of being 'Saturday-night soldiers' to keep in being a vital part of Britain's defence against the day when it was to be needed once more. When the Munich crisis was succeeded by Hitler's march into Czechoslovakia in March 1939 the British government put in hand a number of measures to increase the armed forces, and these included a doubling of the strength of the Territorial Army. This involved each unit of a division creating a 'duplicate' of itself in order to raise, on paper at first, a duplicate division. That of the 51st (Highland) Infantry Division was to be numbered as the 9th (Highland) Infantry Division after the 9th (Scottish) Division of the Great War.

In September 1939 the Territorial Army was mobilised, and a number of divisions were selected to join the regular formations in the British Expeditionary Force; one of these was the 51st (Highland) Division which crossed to France in January 1940. Once established, orders were issued that regular units were to exchange with units from the Territorial divisions in order to 'strengthen' them. In the case of the infantry of the 51st this meant posting out three battalions in exchange for their regular equivalents. This done, the division took under its wing a number of

attached units, with which it now mustered: an armoured car regiment; 13 battalions of infantry (including two machine-gun and two pioneer battalions); six regiments of artillery (four field, one medium, one anti-tank); five companies of engineers; divisional signals; three field ambulances; and supply and ordnance units.

In April 1940 this substantial formation – known as the Saar Force – found itself under command of the French Army in the Metz area holding a section of the Maginot Line. Patrol activities gave the men of the 51st a taste of war and the division its first casualties.

On 10 May 1940 the German Army launched its 'blitzkrieg' attack, striking through Holland and Belgium whilst bombarding the defenders of the Maginot Line, including the 51st (Highland) Division. On the 15th the division began a withdrawal which brought it to the Abbeville area, as part of the French 9th Army, in early June. It was here, on 4 June, that the 51st began a series of battles as its units, by now including several English battalions, fell back on the port of St Valéry-en-Caux, west of Dieppe.

It was the British intention to evacuate the division from Le Havre, and the 154th Infantry Brigade with two field regiments and other attached troops were sent there to secure the port; but when the Germans surrounded the remainder of the division at St Valéry the 154th (now called 'Ark Force') made good their escape to Cherbourg and thence to England.

Meanwhile the Germans were putting pressure on the defensive perimeter around St Valéry while the Royal Navy made attempts to get some of the men of the 51st (Highland) Division away. A savage battle developed until, on 12 June, with all artillery ammunition gone and surrounded by tanks, the GOC, Maj.Gen. Fortune, surrendered the 51st to the German commander, Maj.Gen. Rommel. It was a sad end for a proud division; but one that was to be revenged.

Seven weeks later, in Scotland, the 9th (Highland) Infantry Division was retitled the 51st and its brigades the 152nd, 153rd and 154th. Renumbering of battalions also took place in order to 'perpetuate' some of the battalions which had gone into captivity. Months of hard training followed their reincarnation, and it was not until April 1942 that the 51st moved to Aldershot to prepare for overseas and a return to battle. By now the division was under the command of Maj.Gen. Douglas Wimberley, the leader who was to guide it through its coming battles – a

A private of the Seaforths, 51st (Highland) Division, North Africa, 1942. Note the 'HD' divisional sign *and the Mackenzie tartan patches worn above it and behind the bonnet badge.*

Highland Regts. 1914
1: Lieutenant-Colonel, 5th Seaforth Highlanders
2: Piper, Black Watch
3: Colour-Sergeant, 9th (Highland) Royal Scots

A

Lowland Regts. 1914
1: Lieutenant-Colonel, K.O.S.B.
2: Lance-Corporal, Drummer, Royal Scots Fusiliers
3: Corporal, 6th Highland Light Infantry
4: Privates, Cameronian's
5: Sergeant, Royal Scots

B

9th & 15th (Scottish) Div. 1915
1: Piper Damian Laidlaw, (V.C.)
   7th K.O.S.B., (15th Scottish Div.), 1915
2: Sergeant, 8th Black Watch,
   9th (Scottish) Div., 1915
3: Captain, 12th Highland Light Infantry,
   (15th Scottish Div.), 1915

C

52nd (Lowland) Div. 1915/18
1: Captain, 1/5th K.O.S.B., 1915
2: Drummer, 1/5th Argyll's, 1917
3: Sergeant, 1/6th Highland Light Infantry, 1918

D

9th & 15th (Scottish) Div. 1916/17
1: Sergeant, 8th Black Watch, 1918
2: Sergeant, RGA, (15th Scottish Div.), 1917
3: Lieutenant, 13th Royal Scots,
   (15th Scottish Div.), 1916

1

2

3

E

51st (Highland) Div. 1915/18
1: Corporal, 1/4th Gordon's, 1916
2: Staff Major, 1915
3: Sergeant, 51st Bn. Machine Gun Corps, 1918

F

51st (Highland) Div. 1939/40
1: Pipe-Major, 4th Cameronian's, 1940
2: Captain, Royal Artillery, 1939
3: Private, (LMG gunner)
   8th Argyll's, 1940

G

52nd (Lowland) Div. 1939/44
1: Stretcher-bearer, 6th Highland Light Infantry
2: Company Sergeant-Major of infantry, 1944
3: Piper, 4/5th Royal Scots Fusiliers, 1943

51st (Highland) Div. 1942/44
1: Major-General Wimberley, 1942
2: Colour-Sergeant, 2nd Seaforth's
3: Piper, 5/7th Gordon's, 1943

I

N.W. Europe 1944/45
1: Brigadier Oliver, 1944
2: Brigadier Villiers, 1944
3: Fusilier Donnini, (V.C.)

J

N.W. Europe 1944/45
1: Lieutenant, 2nd Argyll's, (15th Scottish Div.), 1944
2: Private, 5th Seaforth's, (51st Highland Div.), 1944/45
3: Sergeant, 6th Cameronian's, (52nd Lowland Div.), 1945

Insignia
See text for description.

L

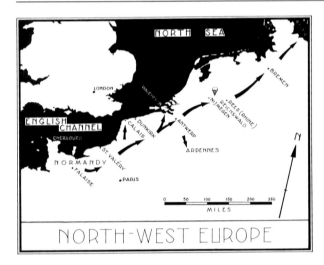

NORTH-WEST EUROPE

man who was fiercely proud of his division, and who did everything possible to promote its special qualities. 'Tartan Tam', as he was affectionately known to his men, insisted on having Scots drafts as reinforcements whenever possible and went to extraordinary lengths to get them, even 'poaching' men from other formations. Under General Wimberley the state of training and morale of the division had been raised to a fine pitch by the time it embarked in June for a destination unknown.

North Africa was to be the battlefield of the 51st (Highland) Division, and it concentrated in Egypt before coming under the command of General Montgomery's 8th Army and moving up to the rear of the El Alamein position. Instruction in desert warfare from the 9th Australian Infantry Division was absorbed, and preparations made for the major British offensive aimed at destroying Rommel's Africa Corps and his Italian allies, and driving them out of North Africa once and for all. Only now, after

two years of see-saw campaigns up and down the North African coastline, did the British have the men and the materials to do so. It was only weeks since the British had stabilised the Alamein position after a series of battles that had halted Rommel's latest advance towards Suez. Montgomery's aim was to force breaks in the enemy's line through which his armour could pass to wreak havoc in the Axis rear areas. The breaks were to be forced by infantry under the protection of a massive artillery barrage, with sappers to clear passages through the enemy minefields.

At 2140 hours on 23 October 1942 the barrage began: almost 1,000 guns crashed out in the greatest concentration of firepower ever seen in Africa, and the sappers and infantry moved over their start lines. One of the four infantry divisions to move forward was the 51st (Highland) Division, its task to seize a five-mile long corridor of desert through which was to pass the 1st Armoured Division.

Led by their pipers, the battalions of the 51st walked steadily forwards into the darkness behind their navigating parties, to meet with a variety of fates. Some made it onto their final objectives; some were held up short of them; but all became embroiled in a savage battle which went on until the night of 27/28 October, when the 51st was relieved by the 1st South African Division. On 2 November the 51st (Highland) Division were back in action in support of the New Zealand Division, capturing the set objectives and throwing off an enemy counter-attack in fine style. Other attacks were put in by the 51st as part of what General Montgomery was to call his 'crumbling' battle until, by the morning of 3 November, it was clear that Rommel's army was withdrawing from its positions; and on the following day Montgomery ordered a pursuit.

The new Highland Division, risen Phoenix-like from

By 1942 the 51st (Highland) Division had reclaimed the famous 'HD' monogram. It was painted on a white ground on vehicles, etc, and was worn in red upon blue for uniform.

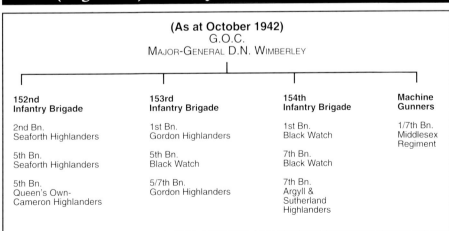

51st (Highland) Infantry Division

(As at October 1942) G.O.C. MAJOR-GENERAL D.N. WIMBERLEY			
152nd Infantry Brigade	**153rd Infantry Brigade**	**154th Infantry Brigade**	**Machine Gunners**
2nd Bn. Seaforth Highlanders	1st Bn. Gordon Highlanders	1st Bn. Black Watch	1/7th Bn. Middlesex Regiment
5th Bn. Seaforth Highlanders	5th Bn. Black Watch	7th Bn. Black Watch	
5th Bn. Queen's Own- Cameron Highlanders	5/7th Bn. Gordon Highlanders	7th Bn. Argyll & Sutherland Highlanders	

Three Black Watch Sergeants of the 51st (Highland) Division, Normandy, August 1944.

Left to right D. Stevenson, A. Dixon and W. Keay. (IWM)

Above: Captain M.Wingate-gray, Black Watch, of the 51st (Highland) Division, organises the evacuation of civilians from Dunkirk. Following appeals by the French Red Cross, a truce was organised to get the 20,000 civilians away before the siege was resumed. October 1944. (IWM)

Below: Universal carriers and 6-pounder anti-tank guns of the 5th Seaforths, 51st (Highland) Division, north of Tilburg, Holland, October 1944. Note the Seaforth battle honour on the carriers side and the '56' above the 'HD' sign at its rear. (IWM)

the defeat at St Valéry, had met the test of its first battle, had participated in a great victory, and had put to flight the army of the victor of St Valéry. Thirty thousand prisoners had been taken by the 8th Army; great numbers of enemy tanks had been destroyed, and immense quantities of war material of all kinds captured. The victory at El Alamein

was to prove to be a turning point; but that was all in the future. Before the defeat of the Axis forces in North Africa the 51st (Highland) Division was called upon to fight again in the battles of Medenine, Mareth, Akarit, Enfidaville and Tunis. It was at Wadi Akarit, on 6 April 1943, that Lt.Col. L. Campbell won the Victoria Cross, leading the 7th Argylls to seize and hold a vital feature.

In July the division landed in Sicily as part of the Allied invasion force, and fought a series of actions in the 39 days it took to secure the island. After the capture of Sicily orders were issued for the 51st to return to the United Kingdom and prepare for another great invasion; Montgomery was going back to command that invasion, and he was taking with him a veteran Corps which included the 51st (Highland) Division. By now an élite formation, the 51st were held in high esteem by the army and by the people of Britain. The 'HD' sign that marked their progress across North Africa and Sicily had earned the men of the division the nickname of the 'Highway Decorators'; and the 6,711 casualties sustained in ten months' fighting were an indication of how hard-won their reputation had been. (At this time, despite the casualties sustained, 80% of the division's officers and 70% of its men were Scots.)

In the June 1944 invasion of Normandy, some units of the division went ashore on 'D'-Day and others followed over the course of the next few days, to be fed into the battle for the beachhead to the east of Caen. By July, and fighting as a division again, the 51st played a part in the operations that led to the breakout from the beachhead and to the entrapment of the German forces at Falaise. In the latter phase units of the division fought without respite for 17 days across 30 miles of country against a determined enemy. Every unit fought at least four main actions.

In September the 51st (Highland) Division, under command of the 1st Canadian Army, returned to St Valéry-en-Caux as liberators, and paid tribute to the original 51st by beating retreat with the massed pipes and drums of the division. Then it was on to Le Havre, where the Germans were holding out to deny the port to the Allies. By 12 September the garrison had surrendered, and units of the 51st moved on to invest the ports of Calais and Dunkirk, still stubbornly held by the Germans.

By mid-October the 51st (Highland) Division was again concentrated and holding a sector of the Nijmegen corridor. On 23 October – the anniversary of El Alamein – operations began to enlarge the corridor and to establish the port of Antwerp as a main supply base. This was the first of a series of battles in the cold, partially flooded countryside of Holland that lasted until December, when the division was called away south.

On 16 December 1944 Hitler launched his armies into an offensive strongly reminiscent of the Germans' desperate gamble of March 1918. Columns of Panzers smashed through the US Army's lines in the Ardennes and pressed westwards towards Brussels and Antwerp. All Allied offensives were cancelled and, in the marshalling of forces to meet the threat, the 51st (Highland) Division was sent

Infantry of the 51st (Highland) Division here the 5th Camerons being carried forward in the Gertogenbosch area, October 1944. (IWM)

to the Laroche area of the Ardennes and placed under command of the 9th US Army. In time the German offensive was contained by the Americans, and the 51st returned north to the British front and the coming offensives that were to lead to the final victory.

The first of these was Operation 'Veritable', which began on the morning of 8 February 1945 with a massive artillery bombardment, behind which the 154th Infantry Brigade – 5/7th Gordons and 7th Black Watch – led the division's assault; 30 Corps were spearheading the 1st Canadian Army's attack on the Reichswald with six infantry divisions, two armoured divisions and three armoured brigades, and the 51st (Highland) Division was in the van. The next ten days saw some of the hardest battles units of the division had fought to date as they pushed on Goch. When the 51st were finally withdrawn from the battle for the Rhineland the scene was set for the crossing of the last great obstacle barring the way to the heartland of Germany – the River Rhine.

At 2100 hrs. on the night of 23 March 1945 the infantry of the 51st began to cross the Rhine at Rees in Buffalo armoured amphibians. There followed 'forty-eight hours of continuous fighting against the most determined enemy we had seen since "D"-Day'. Among the casualties of the Division was the GOC Maj.Gen. Rennie, killed by a mortar bomb while visiting 154th Brigade. A bridgehead established, the 51st was withdrawn from operations in April to rest for a few days before being ordered north into Holland. From here the division began an advance into northern Germany, driving the enemy before it to the Bremen area, where in early May the unconditional surrender of the German forces heralded VE-Day (Victory in Europe day) on 8 May 1945.

It had been a long march for the 51st (Highland) Division, from El Alamein to the Rhine crossing and beyond. Over 15,000 casualties had been sustained in its many battles along the way, and many honours had been won. The 51st remained in Germany on occupation duties until late 1946, when it was 'written off' the order of battle as an active formation, to be re-raised in Scotland as a Territorial Infantry division in 1948.

The 52nd (Lowland) Infantry Division, 1939–45

Like the 51st (Highland) Division, the Lowland Division was re-raised as part of the Territorial Army after the Great War. In 1939 it 'duplicated' itself to create the 15th (Scottish) Infantry Division and, on mobilisation in September of that year, deployed to guard vital areas in Scotland in the opening weeks of the war.

In April 1940 the 52nd (Lowland) Infantry Division moved to southern England, and on 7 June began to move

Men of the 1st Gordons, 51st (Highland) Division, resting after crossing the Maastricht Nord Canal, November 1944. Note the denim overalls being worn over battledress and the PIAT (Projector, Infantry, Anti-Tank) in the foreground. (IWM)

units to France as part of the second British Expeditionary Force. What remained of the first had already been evacuated from the Dunkirk perimeter, minus their heavy equipment. The 51st (Highland) Division was trapped at St Valéry, and such British formations as were south of the Seine were falling back on Cherbourg. It was through this port and others in the region that the British were now landing troops once more to aid their French allies.

After disembarkation the 157th Infantry Brigade (the 5th and 6th HLI and the 1st Glasgow Highlanders) were sent to the Le Mans area and thence to Evreux, where they clashed with advancing German troops on 14 June. The following day the brigade withdrew with the French they were supporting and, on hearing the news of the French appeal for an armistice, fell back to Cherbourg. Here a second British evacuation was in full swing, and the last units of the 52nd were away by 18 June. Thus ended the brief campaign of the 2nd BEF, brought to a premature conclusion by the collapse of the French. Four years were to elapse before a British army returned to France; for the 52nd (Lowland) Division they were to be years of hard training in a variety of roles.

First came the task of defending southern England against the threat of invasion, which seemed so immediate after Dunkirk. The 52nd stood 'on guard' in England and eventually Scotland until the autumn of 1942, when a new role was assigned to it.

A decision was made to raise a 'mountain' division in Scotland – a division equipped, armed and trained to fight in arctic conditions in mountainous country. The 52nd was selected for the task, and settled to it with enthusiasm for the next two years, during which time it represented a real threat to the German northern flank in Europe and helped to tie down large enemy forces in Norway. Special cold weather clothing and equipment were developed and issued to the division; Norwegian liaison units were set up; and the title 'Mountain' was worn below the divisional badge. In time the 'Mountain/Lowlanders' built to a high standard of training and efficiency as they waited for their chance to invade Norway. Plans were drawn up for this eventuality; the King of Norway visited the Division, and a Norwegian brigade took its place alongside the 52nd. Eventually, in June 1944, there came another change of role. (It has since been suggested that the 52nd was used to perpetrate a strategic bluff on the Germans, but at the time of its existence as a mountain division it represented a real and potent threat to them.)

The landings in Normandy saw the 52nd (Lowland) Division training hard in 'combined operations' to fit them for seaborne landings – only to be ordered, in July, to commence training as an 'air-portable' division. In a mat-

Flooding and devastation that followed the assault upon Walcheren by the 52nd (Lowland) Division. (IWM)

Field-Marshal Montgomery talking to a CANLOAN officer serving with the 7th Cameronians, 52nd (Lowland) Division, December 1944. (IWM)

Early in the Second World War the 52nd (Lowland) Division adopted a simplified form of their original sign – the shield of St Andrew only. To this was added a scroll 'Mountain' when the division took up this specialist role.

52nd (Lowland) Infantry Division

(As at October/November 1944)
G.O.C.
MAJOR-GENERAL E. HAKEWELL SMITH

155th Infantry Brigade	156th Infantry Brigade	157th Infantry Brigade	Machine Gunners
7/9th Bn. Royal Scots	4/5th Bn. Royal Scots Fusiliers	5th Bn. Highland Light Infantry	7th Bn. Manchester Regiment
4th Bn. King's Own Scottish Borderers	6th Bn. Cameronians	6th Bn. Highland Light Infantry	
5th Bn. King's Own Scottish Borderers	7th Bn. Cameronians	1st Bn. Glasgow Highlanders	

ter of weeks the units of the division had abandoned the special paraphernalia, skills and organisation acquired in order to fight in the mountains of Norway; had adapted to the life of soldiers who were to invade from the sea; and now had to learn the techniques and limitations of going to battle in the fuselage of a Dakota transport aircraft. The 52nd moved from Scotland to Lincolnshire as part of the 1st Allied Airborne Army, carried out a series of air-move exercises, and waited to be called to the war being waged in north-west Europe. There several airborne operations had been planned and cancelled up to the great 'Market

Garden' venture of September 1944, which saw the 52nd (Lowland) Division standing by to reinforce the British 1st Airborne Division at Arnhem, only to be stood down when the airfield where it was to have landed remained in enemy hands.

When the call finally came it was in none of the specialist roles that the 52nd went to war, neither mountain, nor seaborne, nor air-portable. The division went to war as a standard infantry formation, at a time when both British and American armies in NW Europe were suffering increasing strain from a shortage of infantry after the costly fighting of the summer. In October 1944 the 52nd concentrated in the area of Ghent. Units of the division had had mixed fortunes on their journeys to the rendezvous, especially the 'seaborne echelon' which was caught up in the fighting for the Nijmegen corridor; but now, united once more, they reorganised and refitted for their first battle as a division.

The situation for the Allies at that time was that, if they were to get across the barrier of the Rhine (now that the drive through Arnhem had failed) they had to secure the port of Antwerp and its approaches. These were threatened by the enemy holding Breskens, South Beveland and Walcheren. The task of clearing them out was given to the 1st Canadian Army, under whose command the 52nd (Lowland) Division would serve. By late October the Canadians had cleared the south bank of the Scheldt and the 52nd moved there to embark for the assault on the island of Walcheren and the South Beveland peninsula. Much of the area to be captured had been flooded by the breaching of sea walls with aerial bombing. This led to the rather obvious joke that the division, after training for years to fight in mountains, was to go to war below sea level.

On the evening of 23 October 1944 units of the 156th and 157th Infantry Brigades of the 52nd and specialised armour of the 79th Armoured Division set off to cross the Scheldt and to land on the southern beaches of South Beveland to secure a substantial beachhead. Steady fighting took them inland as reinforcements were landed and a link-up effected with the Canadian forces fighting their way up the isthmus from Antwerp. By the end of the month South Beveland was cleared. Those Germans who had survived the battle withdrew across the causeway to the island of Walcheren, where a strong, determined and heavily-armed garrison awaited the Allied onslaught.

After many attempts to storm the causeway a small bridgehead had been established by the Glasgow Highlanders by 3 November, and this was developed when the 6th Cameronians got over the channel further south. Reinforced by the 5th HLI, a substantial lodgement had been developed by 4 November. Prior to this, on 1 November, the 155th Infantry Brigade and No. 4 Commando had landed at Flushing, and Nos. 41, 47 and 48 Royal Marine Commandos at Westkapelle. The 'softening-up' of the German defences at Walcheren from the air had been going on for days; naval gunfire and artillery shoots completed the bombardment, which had succeeded in knocking out many of the German gun positions. But some remained, and these were turned on the

Men of the 4/5th Royal Scots Fusiliers, 52nd (Lowland) Division, search for snipers in the streets of Stein, Germany, January 1945. (It was in this village that Fusilier Donnini won his posthumous Victoria Cross.) (IWM)

Field-Marshal Montgomery presents the ribbon of the Distinguished Conduct Medal to Sergeant W. Allan of the 4/5th Royal Scots Fusiliers, 52nd (Lowland) Division, January 1945. (IWM)

this position when the Germans launched their Ardennes offensive against the Americans to the south, and units of the division had to stave off a number of German attacks that came their way.

In January 1945 the 52nd (Lowland) Division played a part in the reduction of the Roer 'pocket', a salient of the Siegfried Line that jutted into Allied territory at the juncture of the British and American armies. (It was on 18 January, during these operations, that a soldier of the 4/5th Royal Scots Fusiliers won the Victoria Cross. Fusilier Dennis Donnini was 19 years old and had only been in the army for seven months, the son of an Italian immigrant family settled in Durham. Wounded in the head during the assault on a village, Donnini charged an enemy position and put the occupants to flight with a grenade. He pursued the Germans and, after rescuing a wounded companion, advanced on them firing a Bren gun until wounded a second time. Recovering, Donnini went on firing until a German bullet struck a grenade he was carrying and killed him.) An assault by armoured units on 16 January was followed by an infantry assault two days later, in which all three brigades of the 52nd were engaged in bitter house-to-house fighting to clear a succession of fortified villages, gaining their objectives by 21 January. With the seizure of Heinsberg by the 155th Infantry Brigade on the 24th, the battle for the Roer 'pocket' had been won and the way was clear to contest the Reichwald and to close up to the River Rhine.

Operation 'Veritable' has already been mentioned in connection with the 51st (Highland) Division, and it was through this division that the 52nd passed when, on 14 February 1945, they took up the assault on the British right. A succession of hard battles over the course of the next 24 days culminated in the clearing of the Wesel 'pocket' and brought the division to the banks of the Rhine.

'D'-Day for the crossing of the river was 24 March 1945, and the operation involved all three Scottish divisions: the 15th and the 51st in the crossing, and the infantry of the 52nd to secure the near bank of the crossing place of the 15th, while the artillery of the 52nd added its weight to the massive fire support programme. On 'D'+1 units of the 52nd (Lowland) Division began to cross in support of the 15th (Scottish) Division and 6th Airborne Division, and to join in the fighting to establish the Rhine bridgehead.

This accomplished, the 157th Infantry Brigade was detached in support of the 7th Armoured Division for the fighting advance into Germany. There followed a series of battles to cross water obstacles and capture fortified villages and towns. The 155th Infantry Brigade replaced the 157th with the 7th Armoured Division; the 52nd (Low-

craft bringing the troops to Flushing and Westkapelle, causing casualties afloat and on the beaches. Then began a desperate battle to clear the towns and to press on to Middleburg, which fell to something of a bluff on 5 November when a company of the 7/9th Royal Scots in Buffalo amphibians took the surrender of the German garrison commander and 2,000 of his men.

The first major battle of the 52nd (Lowland) Division in the Second World War had ended in a resounding victory, and the approaches to Antwerp were open. The operations in the Scheldt estuary had truly been 'combined', with the Canadians, Scots and Commandos enjoying support delivered from the air, by sea and by land. There had been many outstanding examples of courage and tenacity shown by troops of the 52nd, including that of the Glasgow Highlanders at the causeway; the 7/9th Royal Scots wading through the floods to storm the Britannia Hotel, Flushing, after a bloody fight; and the cheeky ruse that secured the surrender.

After Walcheren the division went into the line on the British front in Holland, and in December moved to the Geilenkirchen area on the British right. The 52nd held

Prisoners arriving at the 52nd (Lowland) Division cage after the battle for Stein, January 1945. (IWM)

land) Division took under command the 4th Armoured Brigade; and the advance went on, culminating in the battle for Bremen in late April. It was here, in the rubble of the devastated city, that the bugles of the 52nd sounded 'cease fire' on 5 May 1945. The division remained in Germany as part of the forces of occupation until August 1946, when it passed out of existence. In the recreation of the Territorial Army in 1947 the 52nd (Lowland) Division was to have amalgamated with the 51st (Highland) Division to form a single Scottish infantry division. In the event the 51st was raised first, and after an interval the 52nd. Both were disbanded in the reorganisation of the Territorial Army in 1966.

The 15th (Scottish) Infantry Division, 1939–45

The division was the 'duplicate' of the 52nd (Lowland) Infantry Division, born of the decision taken in spring 1939 to double the size of the Territorial Army. The 15th began life officially on 2 September that year, with its units scattered all over the south of Scotland. Like its Great War counterpart the division was short of everything but men. What weaponry and equipment was available was issued to regular and 'first-line' Territorial formations – little was available for the 15th (Scottish) Infantry Division. Nevertheless training of a sort went ahead, and the division played its part in the defence of Great Britain.

In April 1940 a move was made to the south of England where, after the Dunkirk débâcle, the 15th stood guard ready to repel the German invaders expected daily. To do this the division was armed with a 'lower scale' of small arms (just eight light machine-guns per battalion) and a collection of artillery that 'averaged eight museum pieces per regiment'. Digging and wiring were carried out

while the Battle of Britain was being fought in the skies overhead.

Gradually the factories of Britain turned out the weapons, vehicles and equipment needed and the 15th (Scottish) Division was given the tools to do its job properly. Gradually, too, the emphasis of training shifted from defence to mobile operations as 1940 gave way to 1941, a year recorded as being one of progress towards a high standard of efficiency throughout the division. This state of affairs made the blow all the harder when, in November, the order was received that placed the 15th on the 'Lower Establishment'.

By this time, the threat of invasion having receded, the call for reinforcements for the Middle East had grown enormously – particularly armoured reinforcements. To meet the demand certain formations, the 15th (Scottish) Division amongst them, were placed on Lower Establishment and plundered for units and manpower. Ordered to the north of England, the 15th lost two battalions, a field regiment RA, a machine-gun battalion and three minor units, and was drained by incessant demands for drafts of reinforcements for overseas. The maintenance of morale became difficult. Units came and went, including the 7th Camerons, converted to parachutists; the 7th KOSB, converted to glider troops; and the 11th HLI, converted to an armoured role. The atmosphere of 'holding and drafting' made it difficult to maintain a spirit of cohesion. It was therefore with relief that the news was received early in 1943 that the division was to go back onto the Higher Establishment, but this time as a 'mixed' division – basically, an infantry division with one of its infantry brigades replaced by a tank brigade. This arrangement was fairly short-lived; in September 1943, after only six months as a mixed division, the 15th was ordered to reorganise as an infantry division once more.

By now it was obvious to all that the invasion of occupied Europe was only a question of time. Britain was packed with troops for the undertaking, American, British and Canadian, as well as the many 'free' formations from the occupied countries. Much hard training was undertaken as a series of exercises prepared formations for the landings and the breakout from the beachhead. Once again units of the 15th (Scottish) Division moved to the south of England, this time to take their place among the hundreds of thousands of men camped about the ports of embarkation.

'D'-Day came on 6 June 1944 and the lodgement ashore was won; this was the time for the follow-up Corps, which included the 15th (Scottish) Division, to land. By 24 June they were ashore and ready to be sent forward to the battles for which they had been preparing for five long years.

At 0730 hrs. on 26 June the 44th and 46th Infantry Brigades of the 15th crossed their start lines to play their parts in Operation 'Epsom', a two-Corps thrust across the River Orne. The units of the 15th were supported by two battalions of Churchill tanks as well as a variety of special armour, artillery and the divisional machine-gun battalion. Their objective, the River Odon, lay five miles to the south. The bridges over the Odon were to be taken to enable the 11th Armoured Division to sweep across the river to exploit to the south-eastward. Under the thunder of the barrage of several hundred guns the infantry and tanks went forward, in the face of sniper, machine-gun and mortar fire. This enemy reaction caused the men of the 15th to fall behind the barrage, but they pushed on to secure their first objectives. It had been particularly hard fighting on the left, but the objectives had been taken and

were handed over to units of the 43rd (Wessex) Division that night.

The following morning the 227th Infantry Brigade of the 15th took up the advance, and companies of the 2nd Argylls fought their way forward to seize the Odon bridge at Tourmauville, across which poured the lead elements of the 11th Armoured Division. By the third day of the battle all the brigades of the 15th (Scottish) Division were back in the line extending the salient they had won, with the 2nd Argylls capturing another two bridges across the Odon. A battle now developed to clear the road to the Argylls' bridge, but the Germans were still in control of parts of it at nightfall.

The 'Scottish Corridor', as the ground captured by the 15th was now called, was still only 2,500 yards wide and vulnerable to flank attacks. These were launched on 29 June when German counter-attacks were made against the western perimeter of the corridor. They developed at midday and led to savage fighting in which the full arsenal of infantry, armour and artillery weapons was used, but the units of the 15th (Scottish) Division hung on to their gains.

With fresh German Panzer units arriving by the hour it became necessary to move to the defensive, and the armour across the Orne was withdrawn, leaving infantry to hold the ground gained. The 43rd (Wessex) Division was ordered to take over the defence of the eastern sector of the corridor, and infantry from two other divisions were brought forward for possible support.

30 June was a day of reinforcing the 'Scottish Corridor' and repelling German counter-attacks on the 46th

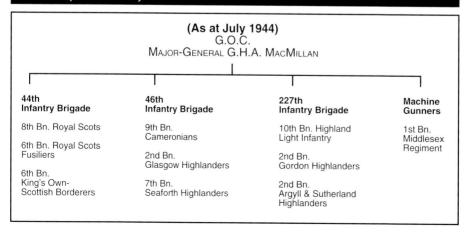

15th (Scottish) Division

		(As at July 1944)	
		G.O.C.	
		MAJOR-GENERAL G.H.A. MACMILLAN	
44th Infantry Brigade	**46th Infantry Brigade**	**227th Infantry Brigade**	**Machine Gunners**
8th Bn. Royal Scots	9th Bn. Cameronians	10th Bn. Highland Light Infantry	1st Bn. Middlesex Regiment
6th Bn. Royal Scots Fusiliers	2nd Bn. Glasgow Highlanders	2nd Bn. Gordon Highlanders	
6th Bn. King's Own Scottish Borderers	7th Bn. Seaforth Highlanders	2nd Bn. Argyll & Sutherland Highlanders	

Once again the 15th (Scottish) Division chose the 15th letter of the alphabet for a sign, but this time with a plain centre. In October 1940 King George VI gave permission for the lion rampant, the Royal Emblem of Scotland, to be placed in the centre of the letter 'O'.

Infantry Brigade and the bridgehead held by the 2nd Argylls; the Argylls took such a battering that they were ordered to withdraw – the bridges at Gavrus were the division's only loss. The enemy attacks continued on 1 July, both south of the Odon and to the western flank of the corridor, where the fighting was heaviest. Elements of five SS armoured divisions were now attempting to break into the 'Scottish Corridor', and against them the British were using 'massed artillery with devastating effect'. Even so the Germans were closing on the infantry positions, and the 6th KOSB was forced to yield ground near Grainville Château.

On 2 July the relief of the 15th (Scottish) Division by the 53rd (Welsh) Division was completed, and the Scots withdrew from their first battle. In the first two days of the five-day slogging match the 15th had driven home a thrust of five-and-a-half miles, and had held its gains against mounting pressure for the next three days. Facing the formidable 12th SS Panzer Division at the start, the division had to contend with elements of the 1st, 2nd, 9th and 10th SS Panzer Divisions and the 21st Panzer Division over the course of the battle: all élite formations led by seasoned veterans at every level. The 15th (Scottish) Division, by contrast, was mainly made up of men experiencing their first battle. Despite this, the 15th had given an excellent account of itself.

The casualties suffered by the division reflected the bitterness of the fighting – 2,720 killed, wounded and missing. The divisional history records that the fighting in Operation 'Epsom', the battle for the 'Scottish Corridor', was to prove to be the fiercest that the 15th (Scottish) Division was to experience in the whole war. Perhaps the best tribute paid to the division was that from their Corps Commander, General O'Connor, who stated: 'I wish to congratulate all most heartily on your recent successful operations. Greatly hampered by weather conditions, which prevented the full employment of our supporting aircraft, you reached your final objectives in the face of fierce opposition. In the subsequent fighting you maintained your positions intact, defeating many enemy counter-attacks. Your courage, tenacity and general fighting qualities have confirmed in battle the high opinion I have always held of you. You have well upheld the highest fighting traditions of Scotland.'

After rest and reinforcement the 15th went back into action when the 44th and 46th Infantry Brigades were put under command of the 43rd (Wessex) Division for a series of attacks aimed at developing the limits of the 'Scottish Corridor' on 10 July.

On the night of 15 July the division spearheaded a thrust south-east from the corridor. Under galling enemy fire, battalions of the 15th (Scottish) Division advanced on

Field-Marshal Montgomery decorating Bombardier H. Moorin, Royal Artillery, with the ribbon of the Distinguished Conduct Medal, September 1944. Note that in the 15th (Scottish) Division all troops, not only the Scottish infantry, wore the 'Tam-o'-Shanter' bonnet. (IWM)

their objectives supported by gun tanks and 'Crocodile' flame-throwing tanks. The first objectives were taken, but the brigades due to take the final objectives became lost, and then came under heavy enemy fire which forced them to dig in short of their objectives. There they fought hard to retain the ground won as a series of German counter-attacks were launched against them. Relieved on 20 July, they had achieved their commander's secondary aim of pulling the enemy armour 'back into the line'.

On 23 July the 15th were moved to the Caumont area to take over from an American formation, and on 30 July took part in the developing break-out battle launched from there. Over the course of the next two weeks the 15th (Scottish) Division fought its way forward to break through the enemy main defences and to create a passage for the British armoured divisions.

In late August the 15th found themselves following up the retreating German forces as they closed up to the River Seine, which was crossed on 28 August. Onward and into Belgium the pursuit continued, across some of the battlefields of the Great War, until mid-September when the 15th relieved the 50th Division in the Gheel bridgehead over the Albert Canal. There bitter fighting took place, especially at Aart, as the great 'Market Garden' airborne operation was fought out. When this failed the front in Holland became somewhat static, and the 15th (Scottish) Division fought a series of battles to develop the

British position up to the river obstacles that had to be crossed.

In February 1945 began the battle for the Rhineland, in which the 15th was given the task of breaking the German Siegfried Line defences north of the Reichswald and the capture of Cleve. The battle began on 8 February and went on for a fortnight, during which the division 'fought itself to a standstill' to achieve the tasks set out for it and more besides.

On 24 March 1945 the leading elements of the 15th (Scottish) Division began to cross the Rhine as part of a massive Allied combined operation that was to strike deep into Germany and bring an end to the war. After linking up with the British 6th and American 17th Airborne Divisions, the 15th fought its way north to develop the bridgehead before being ordered to take part in the advance across Germany. The division battled on, crossing the River Elbe to reach the shores of the Baltic. It was here that the 15th (Scottish) Division's war ended on 5 May 1945 with the unconditional German surrender.

The division remained on occupation duties as units were posted away or disbanded until, on 10 April 1946, the 15th (Scottish) Infantry Division passed into history. It had proved to be a worthy reincarnation of the 15th (Scottish) Division of the Great War, having fought in the crucial battles that gained Allied victory in Normandy, and then leading the drive into Germany after battling up to and across the Rhine. In doing so it had taken 11,772 casualties, killed, wounded or missing; and over 1,300 of its men received honours and awards.

THE PLATES

A: Highland Regiments, 1914:
A1: Lieutenant-Colonel, 5th Battalion, Seaforth Highlanders
A2: Piper, Black Watch
A3: Colour-Sergeant, 9th Battalion, Royal Scots

By 1914 the red coat that had made the British soldier recognisable for two centuries had been relegated to ceremonial use, and drab, or khaki, was the colour for the field. 'Full dress' was never brought back into universal use after the Great War, but the highland regiments retained elements of it with the continued wearing of the kilt and other items of highland uniform.

Figure *A1* depicts a lieutenant-colonel of the 5th (Sutherland and Caithness) Battalion of the Seaforth Highlanders in field uniform. This Territorial unit wore the Sutherland tartan instead of the Seaforth Mackenzie tartan, and had a distinctive bonnet badge behind which officers of various ranks wore different numbers of silver feathers, in this case four. The Glengarry bonnet was worn with service dress, and breeches were cut from regimental tartan.

Figure *A2* shows a piper of the Black Watch (Royal Highlanders) in 'full dress'. The red hackle worn in the feather bonnet was distinctive to the Black Watch, and was later worn in a cut-down form in lieu of a bonnet badge. The tartan worn by Black Watch pipers is Royal Stewart

Major-General C.M. Barber, General Officer Commanding the 15th (Scottish) Division, confers with Brigadier Colville, France, September 1944. The Brigadier had formerly commanded the 2nd Gordons whose badge and title he is still wearing. (IWM)

for the kilt, plaid and pipe-ribbons, and 42nd for the pipe-bag and pipe-ribbons.

Figure A3 shows the 'full dress' of the 9th (Highlanders) Battalion, Royal Scots (Lothian Regiment). A Territorial battalion of a lowland regiment, the 'Dandy Ninth', nevertheless wore the uniform of a highland regiment. The tartan is the Hunting Stewart of the Royal Scots. The badges of rank are for a colour-sergeant, the cuff-stars indicate 20 years' proficiency, and the medals are for South Africa and Long Service.

B: Lowland Regiments, 1914:
B1: Lieutenant-Colonel, King's Own Scottish Borderers
B2: Drummer, Royal Scots Fusiliers
B3: Corporal, 6th Battalion Highland Light Infantry
B4: Private, Cameronians
B5: Sergeant, Royal Scots

The 'full dress' uniform of a lieutenant-colonel of the King's Own Scottish Borderers is depicted in **B1**. The Kilmarnock bonnet had been introduced in 1904 and was worn only by the KOSB and the Royal Scots. Note the black-cocks' feathers; the Leslie tartan; and the medals, which include the Distinguished Service Order, King George V Coronation and the Queen's and King's South Africa medals.

Figure **B2** is a lance-corporal drummer of the Royal Scots Fusiliers in the 'full dress' that only differed from that of an English fusilier in the trews of Government (42nd) tartan, and the Scottish doublet with its gauntlet cuffs and Inverness flaps. Note the drum badge worn on the right arm and the good conduct badges on the left.

B3 shows yet another Territorial uniform eccentricity. The Highland Light Infantry wore trews, but the 6th Battalion wore the kilt in Mackenzie tartan. Note the green Balmoral bonnet, brown leather equipment, and regimental sporran. This corporal wears the badges for Imperial service, 10 to 15 years' efficient service, and medal ribbons for the South African War. His rifle is the magazine Lee-Enfield.

B4 depicts a private soldier of a battalion of the Cameronians (Scottish Rifles) in 'full dress'. Note the trews of Douglas tartan, and the shako and doublet of rifle green. His rifle is the magazine Lee-Enfield. Figure **B5** shows a signalling-sergeant of the Royal Scots (Lothian Regiment) in service dress.

C: 9th and 15th (Scottish) Divisions, 1914/15:
C1: Piper, 7th Battalion, KOSB 15th Division
C2: Sergeant, 8th Battalion Black Watch, 9th Division

C3: Captain, 12th Battalion, HLI, 15th Division
Figure **C1** depicts Piper Daniel Laidlaw, 'the piper of Loos', at the moment of his winning the Victoria Cross with the 7th King's Own Scottish Borderers, 15th (Scottish) Division, on 25 September 1915. The dress that day included gas helmets in lieu of other forms of headdress (Laidlaw, of course, could not have had the protection of his when he played his pipes). The subject is shown in the Royal Stewart kilt worn by pipers of the KOSB; note the kilt apron, 1914-pattern leather equipment, and haversacks for the respirators, smoke helmets and gas goggles carried.

Figure **C2** shows a sergeant of the 8th Battalion, Black Watch (Royal Highlanders), 9th (Scottish) Division, 1915. The subject is in the field service marching order of the 1914-pattern equipment, and is armed with a MkIII short magazine Lee-Enfield. The 8th Black Watch were photographed in this order at Bordon in early 1915. Kilt aprons had yet to be issued, and the old spats and hose were still being worn.

Figure **C3** shows a captain of the 12th Battalion, Highland Light Infantry in late 1915. By now only headdress marked out the lowland regiments as Scottish, and this had become a rather drab Balmoral bonnet. Trench coats and trench boots were the privilege of officers – who bought all their uniform and equipment – and helped to keep out some of the worst of the weather of northern France.

D: 52nd (Lowland) Division, 1915/18:
D1: Captain, 1/5th Battalion KOSB; Gallipoli
D2: Drummer, 1/5th Bn. Argyll & Sutherland Highlanders; Palestine
D3: Sergeant, 1/6th Bn. Highland Light Infantry; Western Front

Tropical uniforms of khaki drill were never issued to the units of the 52nd on the Gallipoli peninsula, the only concession to the sun being the Wolseley helmets issued before embarkation. Figure **D1** depicts a Captain of 1/5th Battalion, King's Own Scottish Borderers at the Helles front. Note the patch of Leslie tartan with stencilled title worn on the helmet pagri, and the cut of the Scottish infantry service dress jacket. Note also the method of wearing the badges of rank on the gauntlet cuff. Troops of the 52nd (Lowland) Division were photographed on Gallipoli wearing webbing equipment; the subject has modified a set of 1908-pattern web to carry a pistol and binoculars.

The only kilted battalions in the 52nd (Lowland) Division were the 1/6th HLI and the 1/5th Argyll and Sutherland Highlanders. A drummer of the Argylls is depicted in the typical uniform worn in Palestine, 1917, as figure **D2**. Note that by now khaki drill jackets were available, and were worn 'cut away' in the Scottish fashion. Plain hosetops and short puttees had replaced spats and coloured hose, although garters were still worn; and the drab serge 'Tam-o'-Shanter' bonnet was the regulation headdress. Our subject is turned out for a quarter-guard.

Figure **D3** shows the uniform of a sergeant of the 1/6th Battalion, Highland Light Infantry in late 1918. The 52nd (Lowland) Division wore a system of coloured bars on the right cuff, the colour denoting the brigade and the number the battalion. This was sometimes painted on the helmet along with the HLI badge. Note the SMLE rifle and bayonet and the No. 5 grenade.

E: 9th and 15th (Scottish) Divisions, 1916/18:
E1: Sergeant, 8th Battalion Black Watch, 9th Division
E2: Sergeant, Royal Garrison Artillery, 15th Division
E3: Lieutenant, 13th Battalion Royal Scots, 15th Division

Figure **E1** depicts a sergeant of the 8th Battalion, Black Watch (Royal Highlanders) in late 1918. In the closing weeks of the war the 9th (Scottish) Division took into use a white metal representation of the divisional sign – a thistle – as a uniform badge, worn on a blue patch on both sleeves. The coloured arcs worn on the shoulders designated the wearer's company: red, A; yellow, B; blue, C; and green, D. The Black Watch had by now adopted the red hackle for wear as a badge in the 'Tam-o'-Shanter' bonnet. Note the 1914-pattern equipment, box respirator and SMLE rifle.

Figure **E2** illustrates the uniform of a sergeant of the Royal Garrison Artillery from one of the trench mortar brigades of the 15th (Scottish) Division, 1917. The divisional sign was often seen painted on the helmets of the divisional artillery, who also wore a patch of Royal Stewart tartan on the sleeve. The sergeant carries a box respirator and wears the belt from the bandolier equipment.

A lieutenant of the 13th Battalion, Royal Scots (Lothian Regiment), 15th (Scottish) Division in 1916 is shown in figure **E3**. Out of the line officers of the lowland regiments wore the Glengarry bonnet and trews illustrated; turn-ups or cuffs on the trews were the height of fashion. The patches of cloth on the sleeves indicated the wearer's company, in this case A. Note the ribbon of the Military Cross; the gold wound stripe on the left cuff; and the ashplant walking stick so favoured by subalterns.

F: 51st (Highland) Division, 1915/18:
F1: Corporal, 1/4th Battalion Gordon Highlanders, 1916
F2: Staff Major, Cameron Highlanders, 1915

F3: Sergeant, Machine Gun Corps, 1918
F1 depicts a corporal 'bomber' of the 1/4th Battalion, Gordon Highlanders at the time of the Ancre battle, 1916. Note the battalion/brigade identification of three light blue bars worn on the sleeves; and the bulky appearance created by the fleece waistcoat, grenade carrier and kilt apron. The equipment is that of the 1914-pattern leather set with respirator haversacks. The grenades carried are the No. 5 pattern, 'Mills bombs', by far the most reliable and widely used by late 1916. Note the bomber's badge on the right sleeve; and the Gordon tartan of the kilt.

Figure **F2** illustrates the uniform of a major on the staff of the 51st (Highland) Division, 1915. Note the retention of most of the uniform of an officer of the Queen's Own Cameron Highlanders, with the addition of staff collar patches and the divisional brassard. The tartan of the breeches is Cameron of Erracht. The medal ribbons are for the coronation of King George V and the Territorial Decoration.

F3 depicts a sergeant of C Company, 51st Battalion, Machine Gun Corps, 1918. Machine-gunners of the 51st continued to wear Scottish headdress after the creation of the MGC, refusing to adopt the service dress cap. The saltire device on the sleeve indicated a machine-gunner, and the colour of company. Other visible insignia include overseas service chevrons, wound stripes and machine-gunner's skill at arms. Equipment is the 1914-pattern leather, box respirator and slung greatcoat. The sergeant is cleaning a Mk6 Webley .455in. revolver.

G: 51st (Highland) Division, 1939/40:
G1: Pipe-major, 4th Battalion Cameron Highlanders
G2: Captain, Royal Artillery
G3: Bren-gunner, 8th Battalion Argyll & Sutherland Highlanders

Figure **G1** shows the pipe-major of the 4th Battalion, Queen's Own Cameron Highlanders in France 1940. This regiment had only recently adopted the blue hackle worn in the 'T-o'-S'. Having been forbidden to wear the 'HD' sign, the 51st (Highland) Division had taken into use a system of saltires and bars which were worn on battledress sleeves to indicate brigade and unit. The tartan is Cameron of Erracht, and the equipment visible is respirator, helmet and 1937-pattern belt.

A captain of one of the Royal Artillery units of the division in 1939 is shown as **G2**. He wears the uniform prescribed for 'the field' including Sam Browne equipment, respirator, helmet, mapcase, binoculars, compass, pistol and haversack. Note the divisional signs worn at this time.

By 1940 the kilt was no longer worn in action. The

Pte. Beale of the 6th KOSB marches towards Loon, Holland, November 1944. Note the patch of Leslie tartan, 15th (Scottish) Divisional sign, and infantry arm-of-service stripe on his sleeve. (IWM)

reasons for this were several, but the main one was the perceived threat of 'mustard' gases, from which the kilt gave no protection. The effect of this was to clothe the highland infantryman in a uniform that was the same as every other British soldier. Figure *G3* shows a light machine-gunner of the 8th Battalion, Argyll and Sutherland Highlanders in the 'battle order' of the time of St Valéry. Note the respirator and the anti-gas cape worn above the pack. The equipment is the 1937-pattern webbing, and the weapon the MkI .303 in. Bren light machine-gun. On the sleeves of the battledress is the device worn by the battalion as the junior in the 154th Infantry Brigade.

H: 52nd (Lowland) Division, 1939/44:
H1: Stretcher-bearer, 6th Battalion Highland Light Infantry, 1940
H2: Company Sergeant Major of Infantry, 1944
H3: Piper, 4/5th Battalion Royal Scots Fusiliers, 1943

Despite orders to the contrary, men of the 6th Battalion, Highland Light Infantry were caught by the camera wearing the kilt in battle during the 2nd BEF period, June 1940. Figure *H1* depicts this uniform, worn by stretcher

bearers. Note the MacKenzie tartan, kilt aprons, coloured hose, and 'SB' stretcher bearer brassards.

Figure *H2* shows the uniform worn in 1944 during the 52nd (Lowland) Division's period as a mountain division. The ski-cap was worn with badges of rank at the front, in this case that of a company sergeant major; and two green bars at the back to indicate a senior NCO/WO – these bars were also worn on the smock hood. The 'wind proof' suit was worn over battledress and FP (Finnish Pattern) boots, and the equipment consisted of a Bergen rucksack and a skeleton assault jerkin. The CSM's weapon is a MkII Sten machine carbine, and he carries snowshoes.

Figure *H3* depicts a piper of the 4/5th Battalion, Royal Scots Fusiliers in 1943; note the divisional and regimental insignia in his sleeve, also the piper's badge. The tartan worn by pipers and drummers in the RSF was Dress Erskine. Pipers were expected to pipe the men of their unit into the charge (most regiments having a nominated piece of pipe music for this occasion), and were therefore armed with pistols for protection in a melée.

I: 51st (Highland) Division, 1942/44:
I1: Major-General Wimberley, 1942

Pte. Baker of the Royal Scots, 15th (Scottish) Division, awaits the order to advance on Meijel, November 1944. (IWM)

I2: Colour Sergeant, 2nd Battalion Seaforth Highlanders
I3: Piper, 5/7th Battalion Gordon Highlanders, 1943

Figure *I1* depicts Major-General Douglas Wimberley, the GOC of the 51st, at the time of the battle of El Alamein. Wimberley was commissioned into the Cameron Highlanders in 1915 and served with the original 51st (Highland) Division in France. He commanded the 1st Camerons in France in 1939/40, and took command of the reconstituted 152nd Infantry Brigade in August 1940. 'Tartan Tam' eschewed the red-banded cap of a general, preferring the Balmoral worn with a general's badge. He is shown wearing the ribbon of the Military Cross and those of the Great War medals on his battledress, as well as the sign of the 51st.

Figure *12* shows the khaki drill uniform worn by a Colour Sergeant of the 2nd Battalion, Seaforth Highlanders when 'out of the line' in North Africa. Note the patch of Mackenzie tartan worn behind the bonnet badge, and on the shoulder straps with the divisional sign.

Figure *I3* depicts a piper of the 5/7th Battalion, Gordon Highlanders, in Tunisia in April 1943. The Gordon tartan, with its distinctive yellow overstripe, is evident on kilt, pipe-bag and ribbons, and on the patches worn on the shoulders and behind the bonnet badge. Note the scrubbed 1937-pattern webbing, with the pistol case worn so as to be clear of the pipes when playing. The Gordon Highlanders traditionally wear 'belled' garters in the style depicted.

J: NW Europe, 1944/45:
J1: Brigadier, 154th Infantry Brigade, 51st Division
J2: Brigadier, 46th Infantry Brigade, 15th Division
J3: Fusilier, 4/5th Bn. Royal Scots Fusiliers, 52nd Division

After their return in triumph from the Middle East the 51st (Highland) Division were often on parade for VIP visitors. Figure *J1* depicts Brigadier James Oliver, commanding the 154th Infantry Brigade, during one such visit. Oliver had commanded the 7th Black Watch in North Africa and Sicily, and preferred its red hackle to a brigadier's badge. Note the badges of rank, collar patches, divisional sign, and the three red bars of the 154th Brigade. The tartan is 42nd, and the badge on the brigadier's sporran is the collar badge of the Black Watch. His medal ribbons are those of the DSO and the Africa Star.

The uniform and insignia worn by Brigadier R.M. Villiers of the 46th Infantry Brigade, 15th (Scottish) Division in 1944 are shown as *J2*. Villiers was a Cameronian, and he retained the Rifle regiment appoint-

ments such as black buttons, arm-of-service stripes and the Cameronians' Douglas tartan patch.

Figure *J3* depicts Fusilier Dennis Donnini VC, of the 4/5th Battalion, Royal Scots Fusiliers. The circumstances of Donnini's award are mentioned in the text. The surviving photographs of this brave young man show him in battledress, proudly wearing the badge of the Royal Scots Fusiliers in his glengarry. The badges shown on his battledress are those worn in the 52nd (Lowland) Division by Donnini's battalion. He did not live to wear the ribbon of the supreme award for gallantry.

K: NW Europe, 1944/45:
K1: Lieutenant, 2nd Bn. Argyll & Sutherland Highlanders, 15th Division
K2: Private, 5th Bn. Seaforth Highlanders, 51st Division
K3: Sergeant, 6th Bn. Cameronians, 52nd Division

Figure *K1* depicts a rifle platoon commander of the 2nd Battalion, Argyll and Sutherland Highlanders, 15th (Scot-

The 1st Middlesex firing support for the 6th Royal Scots Fusiliers at Liesel, Holland, November 1944. The wartime censor has obliterated the insignia of the 15th (Scottish) Division, to which the 1st Middlesex were machine gun battalion. (IWM)

Pipes and drums of the three Scottish Divisions celebrate the victory in the Olympic Stadium, Berlin, November 1945.

tish) Division at the time of the battle for the 'Scottish Corridor' in Normandy. Pictured in battle order, the young lieutenant is armed with a MkIII Sten machine carbine in addition to his pistol. His helmet is well 'scrimmed', and he wears a camouflaged face veil. His equipment is the 1937-pattern webbing, to which he has added an efficient shovel – the infantryman's life-preserver. Note his badges of rank and the insignia of his regiment, division and brigade.

The uniform of a private of the 5th Battalion, Seaforth Highlanders at the time of the German Ardennes offensive is illustrated as **K2**. He is well muffled up against the bitter weather; his clothing includes a leather jerkin and a greatcoat carried on his pack. Note the badge of the 5th Seaforths worn on a patch of Sutherland tartan, which is repeated on his sleeve as a regimental flash. Note also the divisional sign of the 51st (Highland) Division, with the

brigade indicator below. On the march, he carries his 'battle order' webbing, shovel, helmet and No. 4 rifle.

Figure **K3** depicts a sergeant of the 6th Battalion, Cameronians (Scottish Rifles), 52nd (Lowland) Division, 1945. Turned out for one of the many ceremonial occasions that marked the victory in Europe, he wears the 'best suit' of battledress on which all the regimental and divisional insignia were displayed. Note the patches of Douglas tartan, and the ribbons of the Military Medal, 1939–45 Star, France and Germany Star, Defence Medal, War Medal and the Territorial Efficiency Medal.

L: Insignia:

L1 Sign of the 9th (Scottish) Division, worn on uniform 1918. **L2** Sign of the 15th (Scottish) Division, 1917. **L3** Sign of the 51st (Highland) Division ASC, worn on uniform 1918. **L4** 1/7th HLI, 52nd (Lowland) Division,

1918 (lieutenant-colonel). *L5* 15th (Scottish) Division, worn on uniform 1945. *L6* 51st (Highland) Division, worn on uniform 1945. *L7* 52nd (Lowland) Division, worn on uniform 1945. *L8* 'Tam-o'-Shanter', Black Watch, 1918. *L9* Bonnet badges 2nd and 5th Seaforths, 1945. *L10* Bonnet badge, Cameronians. *L11* Bonnet badge, Camerons, 1940. *L12* Khaki drill insignia, lieutenant, Black Watch battalion, 51st (Highland) Division, 1943.

Bibliography

The History of the 9th (Scottish) Division 1914–1919, J. Ewing (Murray, London, 1921)

The 15th (Scottish) Division 1914–1919, J. Stewart & J. Buchan (Blackwood & Sons, Edinburgh, 1926)

The 51st (Highland) Division, F. Farrell (Jackson, Edinburgh, 1920)

The 52nd (Lowland) Division 1914–1918, R. Thompson (Maclehose Jackson, Glasgow, 1923)

The History of the 15th Scottish Division 1939–45, H. Martin (Blackwood & Sons, Edinburgh, 1948)

The History of the 51st Highland Division 1939–45, J. Salmond (Blackwood & Sons, Edinburgh, 1953)

Mountain and Flood: The History of the 52nd (Lowland) Division 1939–46, G. Blake (Jackson, Glasgow, 1950)

Notes sur les planches en couleur

A L'uniforme de parade disparut dans l'ensemble en 1914 et ne réapparut pas de manière universelle dans l'armée britannique. Néanmoins, les régiments des Highlands conservèrent certains éléments de l'uniforme traditionnel pour les parades. A1 Les culottes sont en écossais Sutherland, spécifique à ce bataillon du régiment, tout comme le badge du calot des officiers, le nombre de plumes indiquant le rang. A2 Les cornemuseurs conservèrent généralement leur kilt et autres éléments de l'uniforme de parade. Les cornemuseurs Black Watch portaient un kilt en écossais Royal Stuart. Ceci est l'uniforme de parade tel qu'il était porté en Grande-Bretagne. A3 Uniforme de parade des Highlands porté par un bataillon d'un régiment des Lowlands – le 'Dandy Ninth' – avec un kilt en écossais Hunting Stewart. Les étoiles au revers des manches commémorent 20 ans de service accompli.

B1 Uniforme de parade. Le bonnet Kilmarnock était seulement porté par le KOSB et par les Royal Scots. L'écossais Leslie et les plumes de coq noires sur le bonnet sont des distinctions régimentaires. B2 Uniforme de parade, différent de celui des régiments de fusiliers anglais uniquement par le pantalon en tartan du 42ème écossais et par la coupe en 'doublet' de la tunique. B3 Une autre excentricité de l'uniforme territorial: seul le 6ème bataillon portait le kilt plutôt que le pantalon en tartan. B4 Uniforme de parade des Cameronians, qui marie des éléments Écossais et des Rifles. B5 Sergent des comminications des Royal Scots en uniforme de service.

C1 Le cornemuseur Daniel Laidlaw obtint la Croix Victoria pour avoir joué de la cornemuse sur le parapet sous les tirs ennemis à Loos pour encourager ses camarades démoralisés par le gaz. Notez le kilt Royal Steward sous le tablier de kilt, le matériel de cuir 1914 et les sacs à dos pour le masque à gaz et les lunettes. C2 Feuille de route de service en campagne portée par un sergent du 8ème bataillon, Black Watch, en Grande-Bretagne, 1915. C3 Seul le couvre-chef distinguait maintenant les régiments Lowlands des régiments anglais: le bonnet de Balmoral.

D1 Un uniforme tropical ne fut pas distribué à la 52ème Division à Gallipoli à part le casque Wolseley. D2 Treillis kaki (la veste coupée en style doublet) porté en Palestine, avec le bonnet de serge 'Tam-o'-Shanter', par un tambour en uniforme de garde. D3 Des barres de couleur sur la manchette droite identifiaient maintenant la brigade (par leur couleur) et le bataillon (par leur nombre) dans la 52ème Division. Elles étaient parfois peintes sur le casque, de même quo le badge HLI.

E1 La 9ème division portait le chardon d'argent sur un écusson bleu fin 1918. Des arcs de couleur identifiaient les compagnies dans le 8ème bataillon Black Watch (rouge, jaune, bleu, vert pour A, B, C et D). Les Black Watch portaient une plume rouge au lieu d'un badge de calot. E2 Ce NCO d'artillerie de l'une des brigades mortier des tranchées de la 15ème Division porte, ce qui était typique, le badge de la division sur son casque et un écusson d'écossais Royal Steward à la manche. E3 Hors du front, les officiers des Lowlands portaient le Glengarry et le pantalon en tartan. Notez l'écusson de la compagnie A.

F1 Trois barres bleu clair sur la manche indiquaient la brigade et le bataillon. Notez également le badge de 'bombardier' sur la manche gauche, le gilet en peau de mouton, le porteur de grenades et le kilt en écossais Gordon sous le tablier. F2 Il conserve encore l'uniforme des Cameron Highlanders avec l'addition d'écussons de col rouge et du brassard de la 51ème division. F3 Les mitrailleurs conservèrent le bonnet écossais après la formation du Corps Mitrailleur. L'écusson en sautoir indique un mitrailleur et la couleur sa compagnie. Remarquez également les chevrons rouges du service à l'étranger, la barre doré marquant une blessure et le badge de qualification à la mitraillette.

G1 Ce régiment portait maintenant une plume bleue dans le tam-o'-shanter. La division, qui n'avait pas le droit d'utiliser son signe 'HD', utilisait un système de barres et de sautoirs sur la manche pour identifier les brigades et les unités. G2 Uniforme de campagne prescrit en Grande-Bretagne en 1939. Notez les signes de

Farbtafeln

A Die Paradeuniform verschwand 1914 im allgemeinen von der Bildfläche und kam in der britischen Armee nie mehr zum weit verbreiteten Einsatz. Die Highland-Regimenter behielten jedoch einige Merkmale der traditionellen Uniform für die Parade- und die Ausgehuniform bei. A1 Die Breeches sind aus Sutherland-Tartan und bezeichnend für dieses Bataillon des Regiments, wie auch das Mützenemblem der Offiziere, bei dem die Anzahl der Federn den Dienstgrad angab. A2 Die Dudelsackspieler trugen normalerweise den Kilt sowie andere Elemente der Paradeuniform; die Dudelsackspieler der Black Watch trugen Kilts aus Royal Stuart -Tartan. Hier ist die Paradeuniform abgebildet, wie sie in Großbritannien getragen wurde. A3 Ein Bataillon eines Lowland-Regiments trägt hier die Highland-Paradeuniform mit einem Kilt aus Hunting Stewart-Tartan. Die Sterne an den Aufschlägen stellen die Auszeichnung für 20 Jahre Tüchtigen Dienst dar.

B1 Paradeuniform; die Kilmarnock-Schottenmütze wurde nur vom KOSB und den Royal Scots getragen. Der Leslie-Tartan sowie die schwarzen Hahnenfedern an der Schottenmütze sind Regimentskennzeichen. B2 Paradeuniform, die sich lediglich durch die enganliegenden Hosen im Schottenmuster, nämlich 42ndr-Tartan, und den "Dubletten"-Schnitt des Rocks von der Paradeuniform der englischen Füsilier-Regimenter unterscheidet. B3 Eine weitere Eigenart der Territorial-Uniform: Nur die 6. Bn. trug den Kilt anstelle der enganliegenden Hosen im Schottenmuster. B4 Paradeuniform der Cameronians, die Elemente der schottischen und der Schützenregimenter aufweist. B5 Feldwebel der Fernmeldetruppe der Royal Scots im Dienstanzug.

C1 Der Dudelsackspieler Daniel Laidlaw erhielt das Viktoriakreuz als Anerkennung dafür, daß er zur Ermutigung seiner vom Gas demoralisierten Kameraden in Loos das Partapett unter Beschuß auf und ab seinen Dudelsack spielte. Man beachte den Royal Steward-Kilt unter dem Kilt-Schurz, das 1914er Koppelzeug aus Leder und den Beutel für das Gas-Atemschutzgerät und die Schutzbrille. C2 Marschanzug für den Dienst im Feld, getragen von einem Feldwebel des 8. Bn., Black Watch in Großbritannien, 1915. C3 Die Lowland-Regimenter unterscheiden sich nun lediglich durch die Kopfbedeckung – die Balmoral-Schottenmütze – von den englischen Regimentern.

D1 Abgesehen vom Wolseley-Helm wurde der 52. Division in Gallipoli kein Tropenanzug ausgegeben. D2 Khaki-Drillich – die Jacke im Dubletten-Schnitt – wie in Palästina getragen wurde, mit der "Tam-o'-Shanter" – Mütze aus Serge, hier an einem Trommler im Gardeanzug. D3 Farbige Streifen am rechten Aufschlag kennzeichnen nun die Brigade (durch die Farbe) und das Bataillon (durch die Ziffer) der 52. Division; manchmal wurden die Kennzeichen neben dem HLI-Abzeichen auch auf den Helm aufgemalt.

E1 Ende des Jahres 1918 trug die 9. Division ihre Silberdistel auf einem blauen Ärmelfleck. Farbige Bögen kennzeichneten die Kompanien im 8. Bn. Black Watch – rot, gelb, blau und grün für A, B, C und D. Die Black Watch trugen den roten Federschmuck anstelle eines Mützenabzeichens. E2 Dieser Unteroffizier der Artillerie aus einer der Schützengraben-Mörserbrigaden der 15. Division trägt die Divisionsabzeichen typischerweise auf seinem Helm sowie das Ärmelstück aus Royal Stewart-Tartan. E3 Abseits der Front trugen die Lowland-Offiziere den Glengarry und enganliegende Hosen im Schottenmuster; man beachte das Ärmelstück der Kompanie A.

F1 Drei hellblaue Ärmelstreifen bezeichneten die Brigade und das Bataillon; man beachte auch das "Bomber"-Azeichen am rechten Ärmel, die Schaffellweste, den Granatenträger und den Kilt aus Gordon-Tartan unter dem Schurz. F2 Diese Figur trägt noch die Uniform der Cameron Highlanders unter Zusatz des roten Stabskragenspiegels und der Stabsarmbinde der 51. Division. F3 Nach der Formation des Maschinengewehrkorps behielten die Maschinengewehrsoldaten die

division portés à cette époque. **G3** Le kilt n'était plus porté durant l'action. Ce canonnier Bren se distingue d'un soldat anglais uniquement par le symbole sur la manche du 8ème bataillon A&SH qui est l'unité junior de la 154ème brigade d'infanterie.

H1 Les 6èmes brancardiers HLI furent photographiés en France en juin 1940 portant le kilt contrairement aux orders. **H2** Uniforme et matériel spécialisés portés durant la formation de la 52ème pour en faire une division de montagne. Les barres vertes au dos du calot indiquent un NCO de rang supérieur et le badge de rang CSM est porté à l'avant. L'uniforme 'résistant au vent' se portait avec le treillis et les 'bottes FP', un sac à dos et un squelette de gilet d'assaut. **H3** Insignes de division et de régiment et badge de cornemuseur portés sur la manche. L'écossais est Dress Erskine. Les cornemuseurs portaient un pistolet pour se défendre car ils devient jouer durant l'assaut.

I1 'Tartan Tam' Wimberley, général au commandement de la 51ème division à El Alamein en octobre 1942. **I2** Cet NCO de la 2ème Seaforth, 'hors des lignes' en Afrique, porte un écusson d'écossais Mackenzie derrière son badge de calot et le signe de division sur les épaulettes. **I3** Remarquez l'écossais Gordon, facile à remarquer à cause de sa rayure jaune.

J1 Brigadier Oliver au commandement de la 154ème brigade d'infanterie en Grande-Bretagne avant le débarquement. Remarquez la plume rouge (il dirigea les 7èmes Black Watch dans le désert et en Sicile). **J2** Le Brigadier Villiers de la 46ème brigade d'infanterie conserve ses distinctions Cameronian. **J3** 4/5ème Bataillon, Royal Scots Fusiliers en uniforme de combat avant de s'embarquer pour la France. Le modèle de cette figure est le fusilier D. Donnini, qui mourut par la suite en obtenant la Croix Victoria.

K1 Commandant de section d'infanterie typique en Normandie, fin juin 1944, durant les chauds combats du 'Couloir écossais' contre les unités SS Panzer. **K2** Uniforme d'hiver dans les Ardennes. Remarquez le signe de division, l'écusson d'écossais Sutherland porté comme drapeau de régiment et les rayures de brigade. **K3** Uniforme de cérémonie avec uniforme de combat portant tous ses badges (y compris l'écusson d'écossais Douglas des Cameronians) pour une parade de victoire.

L Insignes – voir les légendes en anglais, qui n'ont pas besoin de traduction.

schottische Kopfbedeckung bei. Das schrägkreuzförmige Ärmelstück bezeichnet den Maschinengewehrschützen, die Farbe seine Kompanie; man beachte auch die roten Winkel des Auslandsdienstes, das goldene Verwundetenabzeichen und das Maschinengewehr-Eignungsabzeichen.

G1 Inzwischen trug das Regiment einen blauen Federschmuck an der "Tam-o'-Shanter"-Mütze. Die Division, der die Verwendung ihres "HD"-Zeichens verboten war, benutzte eine Reihe von Streifen und Schrägkreuzen auf dem Ärmel zur Kennzeichnung der Brigade und der Einheit. **G2** Die vorschriftsmäßige Felduniform, wie sie 1939 in Großbritannien getragen wurde – man beachte das Divisionsabzeichen, das zu dieser Zeit getragen wurde. **G3** Im Gefecht wurde der Kilt nicht mehr getragen; dieser Bren-Schütze unterscheidet sich von einem englischen Soldaten lediglich durch das Ärmelemblem des 8. Bn. A&SH als subalterne Einheit der 154. Infanteriebrigade.

H1 Krankenträger des 6. HLI wurden im Juni 1940 in Frankreich fotografiert, wo sie entgegen den Vorschriften Kilts trugen. **H2** Spezialanzüge und -ausrüstung, die die 52. Division bei der Ausbildung als Gebirgsjägerdivision trugen; grünen Streifen auf der Rückseite der Mütze kennzeichnen einen dienstälteren Unteroffizier, das Rangabzeichen des Kompanie-Hauptfeldwebels befindet sich auf der Vorderseite. Der "windundurchlässige" Anzug wurde mit dem Kampfanzug und den "Stiefeln finnischen Musters" getragen, sowie einem Rucksack und einer notdürftigen Kampfweste. **H3** Die Divisions- und Regimentsabzeichen sowie das Abzeichen des Dudelsackspielers befinden sich auf dem Ärmel; bei dem Tartan handelt es sich um Dress Erskine. Die Dudelsackspieler hatten zur Selbstverteidigung Pistolen bei sich, da sie während des Gefechts spielen mußten.

I1 "Tartan Tam" Wimberley, kommandoführender General der 51. Division, in El Alamein im Oktober 1942. **I2** Dieser Unteroffizier der 2. Seaforth, "abseits der Front" in Afrika, trägt ein Stoffstück aus Mackenzie-Tartan hinter seinem Mützenemblem und dem Divisionsabzeichen auf den Schulterklappen. **I3** Man beachte den charakteristischen Gordon-Tartan mit dem gelben Streifen.

J1 Brigadier Oliver, Befehlsführer der 154. Inf. Bde. in Großbritannien vor dem D-Day; man beachte den roten Federschmuck – er führte die 7. Black Watch in der Wüste und in Sizilien an. **J2** Brigadier Villiers der 46. Inf. Bde. trägt noch die Merkmale der Cameronians. **J3** Kampfuniform der 4./5. Bn., Royal Scots Fusiliers, vor dem Aufbruch nach Frankreich. Modell für diese Figur stand Füsilier D. Donnini, der später fiel und das Viktoriakreuz erhielt.

K1 Typischer Infanterie-Zugführer in der Normandie, Ende Juni 1944, während des erbitterten Kampfes um den "schottischen Korridor" gegen die Panzereinheiten der SS. **K2** Winteranzug in den Ardennen. Man beachte das Divisionsabzeichen, das Stoffstück aus Sutherland-Tartan, das als Regimentsabzeichen dient, und die Kennstreifen der Brigade. **K3** Anzug für Zeremonien mit Kampfanzug mit allen Abzeichen (einschließlich des Stoffstückes aus Douglas-Tartan der Cameronians) für Siegesparaden.

L Abzeichen – siehe Bildunterschriften in englischer Sprache, die für sich selbst sprechen.